D1361488

The Speaker's Treasury
of 400 Quotable Poems

The "Sourcebook" Series:

The Speaker's Sourcebook
   Compiled by Eleanor Doan

Robert G. Lee's *Sourcebook of Illustrations*

The Speaker's Treasury of 400 Quotable Poems
   Compiled by Croft M. Pentz

The Speaker's Treasury of 400 Quotable Poems

compiled by

CROFT M. PENTZ

ZONDERVAN PUBLISHING HOUSE
GRAND RAPIDS, MICHIGAN

Dedicated
To My Mother,
whose prayers, life and example
brought me to Christ.

Introduction

Next to the Holy Scriptures, poetry has helped mankind more than anything I know. Poetry has brought many glorious climaxes to messages. Poetry has comforted many bereaved people through the ages. Poetry has cheered the lonely. Poetry has given hope to the hopeless. Yes, there is no limit to the power of Christian poetry.

These poems were taken from various sources. To the best of my knowledge, all copyrighted material is credited. The poems of Annie Johnson Flint are used by permission of Evangelical Publishers (see Index by Author for listing). Mrs. Martha Snell Nicholson's poem, "Home," is used by permission of Moody Press. Singspiration, Inc. graciously granted permission to use "Yes, I Have Been to Calvary" by Avis B. Christiansen, and "Have I Done My Best for Jesus?" by Ensign Edwin Young.

It is my prayer that these poems will be a blessing to you as they have been to me.

Proceeds from this book will go to help enlarge the Assemblies of God Missions to the Deaf in the greater New York area.

CROFT M. PENTZ

TABLE OF CONTENTS

The Speaker's Treasury of 400 Quotable Poems

The Bible

MY COMPANION

When quiet in my room I sit,
  Thy Book be my companion still;
My joy Thy sayings to repeat,
  Talk o'er the records of Thy will,
And search the oracles divine,
  Till every heartfelt word is mine.

Charles Wesley

THE WORD OF GOD

I love Thy Word, O God:
  Its pages brightly shine,
A beacon light along the road
  That leads to truth divine.

I love Thy Word, O God:
  For comfort freely given;
For inner peace that keeps my soul,
  And gives me thoughts of heaven.

I love Thy Word, O God:
  For songs of purest joy,
That fill this pilgrim heart of mine,
  And lips of praise employ.

I love Thy Word, O God:
  That tells me of Thy Son;
Of His redemption on the cross
  For needy sinners won.

I love Thy Word, O God:
  It ne'er shall pass away,
Till earth's dark night of sin shall turn
  To God's own perfect day.

J. Harold Gwynne

READ THE BIBLE THROUGH

I supposed I knew my Bible,
  Reading piecemeal, hit or miss,
Now a bit of John or Matthew,
  Now a snatch of Genesis.
You who treat the crown of writings
  As you treat no other book —
Just a paragraph disjointed,
  Just a crude impatient look —
Try a worthier procedure!
  Try a broad and steady view.
You will kneel in very rapture,
  When you read the Bible through!

Amos R. Wells

THE BIBLE

There is wisdom in the Bible
  That all science cannot know;
There we find strong men of courage
  As they seeds of Gospel sow,
There are poetry, and beauty,
  And wise parables that tell
In most simple words, great wisdom;
  We should read, and heed them well!

There is glory in the Bible!
  All creation sings God's praise;
We find help, and strength and courage
  For the roughest earthly ways;
There is comfort for the lonely,
  There is peace for tempest-tossed;
There is rest for those aweary;
  And our Saviour paid its cost!

Dorothy Conant Stroud

11

MY BIBLE AND I

We've traveled together through life's
    rugged way,
O'er land and o'er water, by night and
    by day;
To travel without it I never would try;
We keep close together, my Bible and I.

In sorrow I've proved it my comfort and
    joy;
When weak, my strong tower which
    nought can destroy
When death comes so near me 'tis
    thought I would die,
We still are together, my Bible and I.

If powers of evil against me would come,
And threaten to rob me of heaven and
    home,
God's Word then directs me to Him in
    the sky;
And nothing can part us, my Bible and I.

When evil temptations are brought to my
    view,
And I in my weakness know not what
    to do,
On Christ as my strength I am taught to
    rely;
We conquer together, my Bible and I.

When life's path is ended — if Jesus
    should come,
And take all His Blood-purchased
    brethren home,
Or if, in longsuffering, He waits till I
    die —
We'll never be parted, my Bible and I.

With all His redeemed gathered safe in
    the fold,
And when in the glory my Lord I behold,
My Bible and I close companions will be,
For God's Word abides for all eternity.

MY OLD BIBLE

Though the cover is worn,
    And the pages are torn,
And though places bear traces of tears,
    Yet more precious than gold
    Is this Book worn and old,
That can shatter and scatter my fears.

    This old Book is my guide,
    'Tis a friend by my side,
It will lighten and brighten my way;
    And each promise I find
    Soothes and gladdens the mind,
As I read it and heed it each day.

    To this Book I will cling,
    Of its worth I will sing,
Though great losses and crosses be mine;
    For I cannot despair,
    Though surrounded by care,
While possessing this blessing divine.

GOD'S TREASURE

There is a Treasure,
Rich beyond measure,
    Offered to mortals today;
Some folk despise it,
Some criticize it,
    Some would explain it away.

Some never read it,
Some never heed it,
    Some say "It's long had its day";
Some people prize it,
And he who tries it
    Finds it his comfort and stay.

God gave this Treasure,
Rich beyond measure,
    His Word, we call it today.
Let us believe it,
Gladly receive it,
    Read, mark, and learn to obey.

A. M. N.

THE ANVIL OF GOD'S WORD

I stood one day beside a blacksmith's
    door,
    And heard the anvil ring the vesper
    chime;

Then, looking in I saw upon the floor
    Old hammers, worn with beating years
    of time.

"How many anvils have you had?" said I,
    "To wear and batter all these hammers
    so?"

"Just one," he said, then said with
    twinkling eye,
    "The anvil wears the hammers out,
    you know."

And so methought the anvil of God's
    Word.
    For ages skeptics' blows have beat upon

And though the noise of falling blow was
    heard,
    The anvil is unharmed, the hammers
    gone.

BELIEVE THE BIBLE

There are some who believe the Bible,
And some who believe in part,
And some who trust with a reservation,
And some with all their heart.
But I know that its every promise
Is firm and true always;
It is tried as the precious silver,
And it means just what it says.
It is strange we trust each other,
And only doubt our Lord;
We will take the word of mortals,
And yet distrust His word;
But, oh, what light and glory
Would shine o'er all our days
If we always would remember
That He means just what He says.
A. B. Simpson

The Blood

IN MY PLACE

Thy Blood was shed for me,
    My life belongs to Thee.
With Thee I died, with Thee I rose.
    Thou livest now in me.

Thy body bruised for me.
    How can I thankless be,
Or hesitate to offer mine
    A sacrifice to Thee?

Blood from Thy thorn-pierced brow
    Washed my vile thoughts away.
Take captive ev'ry thought, O Christ,
    And teach them to obey.

Blood from Thy nail-pierced hands
    Cleansed all my evil deeds.
Now use my strength in youth, my Lord,
    To sow Thy precious seed.

Thy feet were pierced with nails
    Because mine went astray.
Lord, keep me walking in the light
    Of Thine eternal way.

Thy back was lashed that mine,
    Bent low beneath my sin,
Might lose its load at Calvary
    And I the race might win.
Esther Archibald

THE PRECIOUS BLOOD

When the enemy surrounds you,
    coming on you as a flood,
And the fiery darts beset you,
    that's the time to plead the Blood.

When your task seems much too heavy,
    and you are misunderstood,
Let this be your pledge and token,
    There is power in Jesus' Blood.

When life brings you only losses
    and withholds from you the good,
Just rejoice to bear the crosses;
    trusting Jesus' precious Blood.

As you live your life's short story,
    for each problem, thought or mood,
All sufficient is the glory
    of the Lord's atoning Blood.

Herald of Holiness

Calvary

WE'LL NEVER KNOW

We'll never know what suffering
    Our Saviour had to bear
When He, upon that cruel cross
    In shame did die up there;
But this we know, our debt was paid
    Upon that cross of woe,
When God upon His Son outpoured
    His wrath, so long ago.

We'll never know the price He paid
    To take away our sin,
When He went down into the depths
    Where none had entered in;
But this we know, God punished Him
    To pardon you and me;
And now God's claims are met,
    We can from guilt be free.

We'll never know how great God's love
    Drew from His heart this plan,
That brought the Saviour from above
    To die for sinful man;
But this we know, He loves us still
    And seeks us in His grace,
That with the Son of His dear love,
    In heav'n we have a place.

A. Hoellein

THY NAIL-PIERCED HANDS

Jesus, my Lord, when I look upon Thee
And Thy nail-pierced hands fast to the
    tree,
All wretched pride melts 'neath Thy
    cross;
Things of this world become as dross.

Jesus, My Lord, when I look upon Thee
And Thy nail-pierced hands outstretched
    toward me,
All self desires melt 'neath Thy gaze;
One desire looms: Thine, Lord, always!

Jesus, my Lord, when I look upon Thee
And Thy nail-pierced hands broken for
    me,
Things of this world grow dimmer still;
One wish remains: Master, Thy will!

Jesus, my Lord, when I look upon Thee
And Thy nail-pierced hands bleeding
    for me,
This heart and soul melt 'neath such love;
Jesus, my Lord, sent from above.

Kathryn Bowsher

14

IN MEMORY OF TWO SONS

Somewhere upon a battlefield,
  In a war of bygone years,
One of our nation's brave sons fell,
  And brought a mother's tears;
An unsung hero of our land
  Died so we might be free,
I'd like to take his hand in mine,
  Say, "Thanks, you died for me,
Though some may soon forget, by one
  You shall remembered be."

Somewhere upon a lonely hill,
  On a rugged cross of wood,
Another Son laid down His life —
  The precious Son of God;
Somewhere in heaven up above
  It brought a Father's tears,
And so He knows that mother's heart,
  Oh yes, He knows and cares,
Did He not soothe her deepest grief,
  And calm her anxious fears?

And through the death of His dear Son,
  By the sacrifice He made,
Our freedom from all sin was won,
  The debt was fully paid;
I'd like to take His hand in mine,
  Say, "Christ, you died for me,
I thank you for your suffering
  Upon the cruel tree,
Though others may perhaps forget,
  I give my all to Thee."

Russell Stellwagon

IT WAS FOR ME

He died for me, my Saviour, He,
The blessed Lamb of Calvary;
Upon the cross He set me free,
'Twas there He died to ransom me.

In heaven now, it is for me
He intercedes so pleadingly;

And soon He'll come again for me
In clouds of light, my Bridegroom be.

And then forevermore I'll be
With Him, my Lord, eternally;
O glorious day, eternity
With Him, the blessed One in Three.

Eva Gray

BEHOLD THE MAN!

O thorn-crowned brow,
  Upon my Lord and King!
O Saviour Thou,
  A purple robe they bring
And mock my Lord
  As out they cry:
(The cruel, wicked throng)
  "Him Crucify!"
That one who did no wrong,
  My lovely Lord.

They hail Him King,
  And smite Him with the hand
Of smart and sting;
  Saith one, "Behold, the man!"
It was my Lord
  Who stood alone
In Pilate's hall of doom;
  'Twas ever known
He'd stand there in my room,
  My Saviour, Lord.

The cross He bore
  Upon Mount Calvary,
The crown He wore,
  Was for His love for me;
Yes, Christ my Lord
  Was crucified
Because He loved me so;
  He bled and died
To pay the debt I owe,
  My God and Lord.

Rod of God

15

THE CRADLE AND THE CROSS

When Bethlehem's manger first cradled
the King,
And angels glad news to the shepherds
did bring,
The blackness of midnight beamed like
the sun,
As God gave to mankind His wonderful
One.

But when on the cross, as a sinner, Christ
died,
With nail-pierced hands, and with
spear-riven side,
The brightness of noonday was turned
into night,
And men smote their breasts at the
sorrowful sight.

Yet Bethlehem's cradle and Calvary's
hill
Were all in the plan of God's infinite
will.
The cross and the manger were made for
this King
And heaven forever His praises will
sing.

Today, Christ the light of the world will
come in
And cleanse any heart from its
midnight of sin.
His presence will banish the darkness of
night,
And brighten the soul with His
heavenly light.

All hail then to Jesus, our Lord evermore,
As men of all nations the Saviour
adore.
To Bethlehem's Infant, to Calvary's King,
Our deepest devotion and homage we
bring.

A. S. Reitz

GETHSEMANE

'Tis midnight — and on Olive's brow,
The star is dimmed that lately shone;
'Tis midnight — in the garden now
The suffering Saviour prays alone.

'Tis midnight — and, from all removed,
Immanuel wrestles, lone with fears;
E'en the disciple that He loved
Heeds not his Master's grief and tears.

'Tis midnight — and for other's guilt
The man of sorrows weeps in blood;
Yet He, who hath in anguish knelt,
Is not forsaken by His God.

'Tis midnight — and, from ether-plains,
Is borne the song that angels know;
Unheard by mortals are the strains
That sweetly soothe the Saviour's woe.

W. B. Tappan

THEY CRUCIFIED MY LORD

They nailed my Saviour to the cross,
The cross on Calvary;
'Twas there in agony He died
For sinful souls like me.

They placed upon His brow a crown,
A cruel crown of thorn;
Placed it upon that gentle brow,
In bitter hate and scorn.

Despised, rejected, loving still,
My dear Lord suffered there;
"Forgive, they know not what they do,"
His tender dying prayer.

How can I show my love to Him
Who suffered thus for me?
All that I have — a humble gift
His evermore shall be.

HE WAS NOT WILLING

"He was not willing that any should
  perish";
  Jesus enthroned in the glory above,
Saw our poor fallen world, pitied our
  sorrows,
  Poured out His life for us — wonderful
  love!
Perishing, perishing! Thronging our
  pathway,
  Hearts break with burdens too heavy
  to bear,
Jesus would save, but there's no one to
  tell them
  No one to lift them from sin and
  despair.

"He was not willing that any should
  perish";
  Clothed in our flesh with its sorrow
  and pain,
Came He to seek the lost, comfort the
  mourner,
  Heal the heart broken by sorrow and
  shame.
Perishing, perishing! Harvest is passing,
  Reapers are few and the night draweth
  near,
Jesus is calling thee, haste to the reaping,
  Thou shalt have souls, precious souls
  for thy hire.

Plenty for pleasure, but little for Jesus;
  Time for the world, with its troubles
  and toys,
No time for Jesus' work, feeding the
  hungry,
  Lifting lost souls to eternity's joys.
Perishing, perishing! Hark, how they call
  us;
  "Bring us our Saviour, oh, tell us of
  Him!

We are so weary, so heavily laden,
  And with long weeping our eyes have
  grown dim."

"He was not willing that any should
  perish";
  Am I His follower, and can I live
Longer at ease with a soul going down-
  ward,
  Lost for the lack of the help I might
  give?
Perishing, perishing! Thou wast not
  willing;
  Master, forgive, and inspire us anew;
Banish our worldliness, help us to ever
  Live with eternity's values in view.
                              Lucy R. Meyer

AT THE CROSS

My heart dissolved to see Thee bleed,
  This heart so hard before;
I hear Thee for the guilty plead,
  And grief o'erflows the more.
'Twas for the sinful Thou didst die,
  And I a sinner stand;
What love speaks from Thy dying eye,
  And from each pierced hand!

I know this cleansing blood of Thine
  Was shed, dear Lord! for me;
For me, for all — oh! Grace Divine!
  Who look by faith to Thee.
O Christ of God! O spotless Lamb!
  By love my soul is drawn;
Henceforth, for ever, Thine I am;
  Here life and peace are born.

In patient hope the cross I'll bear;
  Thine arm shall be my stay;
And Thou, enthroned, my soul shall
  spare,
  On Thy great judgment-day.

17

YES, I HAVE BEEN TO CALVARY
(Inscribed to Rosemary Zylstra)

While here on earth it may not be
My privilege to view
The sacred spots in Galilee
Which Christ, my Saviour, knew.
I may not tread the hallowed paths
He travelled day by day,
Nor worship on that holy mount
Where oft He knelt to pray.

But on the wings of faith, praise God,
I've been to Calvary,
And 'neath that precious, cleansing flood
From sin I've been set free!

My eager eyes may never see
The streets of Bethlehem,
Or Nazareth or Bethany —
Or e'en Jerusalem.
It may not be my joy to tread
On yonder peaceful shore,
Where Christ with Living Manna fed
His followers of yore.

I may not stand in silent awe
Within that garden wall,
Where Jesus agonized in prayer,
And yielded up His all.
Nor may I gaze upon the tomb
Wherein His body lay,
Till joy divine dispelled the gloom,
And night was turned to day.

Ah yes, though I may ne'er behold
Those scenes I dearly love.
Some day I'll walk the streets of gold
With Christ, my Lord, above!
For soon He's coming back again
In pow'r and majesty,
And I shall go with Him to dwell
For all eternity!

Avis B. Christiansen

HE GAVE HIMSELF FOR ME

While standing on the brink of woe,
I saw Mount Calvary,
Where Jesus full atonement made;
He gave Himself for me.

His dying there my debt has paid —
Forever sets me free,
From all the guilt of Adam's race.
He gave Himself for me.

And gazing on that wondrous scene —
My sins nailed to the tree,
Could scarce believe the sight I saw,
He gave Himself for me.

When I am safe on heaven's shore,
My portion there will be,
To sing throughout eternal years,
He gave Himself for me.

WONDROUS SON OF GOD

He who hung on Calvary's tree,
After dark Gethsemane,
Died for me, for me!
Wondrous Son of God.

Hands that threw the world in space
Cruel men did so debase;
Nail prints show He took my Place —
Wondrous Son of God.

All who put their trust in Him,
He will cleanse from every sin;
So help another soul to win
To the Son of God.

Oh, what mercy and what grace,
For the fallen human race!
Someday we'll behold His face —
Wondrous Son of God.

Berniece Goertz

O SON OF GOD, AFFLICTED

O Son of God, afflicted,
And slain for sinful men,
My soul hath oft depicted
What Thou didst suffer then,
The pain, the grief, the sighing,
The burden of Thy woe,
The cross, the shame, the dying
That filled Thy life below.

Ah, why from heavenly blessing
Didst Thou to earth descend,
And share the woes distressing,
To be the sinner's Friend?
The angels looked amazed,
While men untouched beheld
The Christ to souls debased,
By love divine impelled.

'Twas love, 'twas love unbounded,
As high as heaven ascends,
As deep as depths unsounded,
And broad as earth extends;
Yea, 'twas a love undying,
That suffered for my sake;
Lord, may a love replying,
Within my soul awake.

Translated
from the Greek by
John Brownles D.D.

THE LAST DAY

I can close my eyes and see Him
As He lived that last sad day,
Spat upon, despised, rejected,
Walking on, Golgotha-way.

How His heart must have been breaking
As they jeered and laughed to scorn,
Even though He knew this hour
Was the reason He'd been born.

Oh, the pain He must have suffered
Hanging on that cruel tree!
I will never cease to marvel
That He bore all this for me.

But the shame was changed to glory
On that first bright Easter Day,
As He arose in shining triumph
To immortalize this clay.

Lola Derosier

CRUCIFIXION

If we had lived on that long-gone day
When they nailed Him to the tree,
Do you suppose that you and I
Would have led Him to Calvary?

Would we have joined the jeering throng
That clustered at His feet;
Would we have mocked Him, spat upon
His face, so calm and sweet?

Would we have stood complacently
To see Him crucified;
To see His nail-pierced hands and feet,
His crown of thorns, His wounded side?

Ah, no! Such shame would not be ours
We say, and yet — and yet —
So often in the stress of Life
My friend, do we forget —

That long steep hill, the angry mob,
The crosses, stacked against the sky,
The gentle Man, so kind, so brave,
Going forth, alone, to die!

We would not crucify Him once,
And yet so sinful is our way,
So blind are we, and selfish, too,
We crucify Him every day!

Mrs. Roy L. Peifer

19

SCARRED

The shame He suffered left its brand
In gaping wound in either hand;
Sin's penalty He deigned to meet
Has torn and scarred His blessed feet;
The condemnation by Him borne
Marred His brow with print of thorn.
Trespass and guilt for which He died
Have marked Him with a riven side.

IN CHRIST

In Christ there is no East nor West,
  In Him no South nor North,
But one great fellowship of love
  Throughout the whole wide earth.

In Him shall true hearts everywhere
  Their high communion find;
His service is the golden cord
  Close binding all mankind.

Harvest Field

I SAW ONE HANGING

I saw one hanging on a tree,
  In agonies and blood,
Who fixed His languid eyes on me,
  As near His cross I stood;

Sure never to my latest breath,
  Can I forget that look;
He seemed to charge me with His death,
  Though not a word He spoke.

My conscience felt alone my guilt
  And plunged me in despair;
I saw my sins His blood had spilt
  And helped to nail Him there.

A second look He gave, which said,
  "I freely all forgive;
My blood is for thy ransom paid,
  I die that thou mayest live."

Christian Living

ATTRACTION

Christ will prove the true attraction
  When a sinner feels his need,
When he sees in every action
  Nothing in God's court to plead.

When a sinner, judgment knowing,
  Wants a Saviour who can save,
Then, from human efforts going,
  For free mercy will he crave.

Christ will prove the true attraction,
  He will save the sinner lost!
Law demanded its full action,
  But the Saviour met the cost.

Wondrous mercy now outshining,
  Shows redemption's work is done,
And no more in death repining,
  We are welcomed in God's Son.

Christ is still the one attraction,
  To each child of God made nigh.
Other names and schemes cause faction,
  How can we on men rely?

His the name, Himself the center,
  His the glory when we meet,
In Himself by grace we enter,
  Where there is the mercy seat!

LIFE'S LESSONS

I learn as the years roll onward
And I leave the past behind,
That much I had counted sorrow
But proves that God is kind;
That many a flower that I longed for
Had hidden a thorn of pain,
And many a rugged by-path
Led to fields of ripened grain.

The clouds that cover the sunshine,
They cannot banish the sun,
And the earth shines out the brighter
When the weary rain is done.
We must stand in the deepest shadow
To see the clearest light;
And often through wrong's own darkness
Comes the living strength of light.

The sweetest rest is at even,
After a wearisome day,
When the heavy burden of labor
Has been borne from our hearts away;
And those who have never known sorrow
Cannot know the infinite peace
That falls on the troubled spirit
When it sees at last release.

We must live through the dreary winter
If we would value the spring;
And the woods must be cold and silent
Before the robins sing.
The flowers must be buried in darkness
Before they can bud and bloom,
And the sweetest, warmest sunshine
Comes after the storm and the gloom.

YOU CAN'T FOOL GOD

You can fool the hapless public,
You can be a subtle fraud,
You can hide your little meanness,
But you can't fool God!

You can advertise your virtues,
You can self achievement laud,
You can load yourself with riches,
But you can't fool God!

You can criticize the Bible
You can be a selfish clod,
You can lie, swear, drink, and gamble,
But you can't fool God!

You can magnify your talent,
You can hear the world applaud,
You can boast yourself somebody,
But you can't fool God!

Grenville Kleiser

REMINDER

It's funny how a little thing
Can set a person thinking;
Can lift the load of weariness,
When eyes with tears are blinking.

Why, it was only yesterday
A little sparrow's cheeping
Reminded me of the Father's love,
And banished all my weeping.

I'd thought my world had fallen through,
And all my hopes were broken,
Until I heard his cheery chirp,
And through it Christ had spoken.

To tell again of wondrous love
To featured folk and lily;
And here was I, worth more than they,
And nearly worried silly.

I asked forgiveness for my sin,
And soon the clouds had drifted;
And with my little feathered friend
My voice in praise had lifted.

EVER ON

Growing old but not retiring,
  For the battle still is on;
Going on without relenting
  Till the final victory's won.
Ever on, nor think of resting,
  For the battle rages still,
And my Saviour still is with me
  And I seek to do His will.

Years roll by, the body weakens,
  But the spirit still is young;
Breath of God — it never ages,
  Is eternal, ever strong.
Rather, year by year it strengthens,
  Gaining o'er the things of sense.
By Thy Spirit, lead my spirit,
  Saviour, till Thou call me hence.

Things of earth decrease in value,
  Brighter shines the light above;
Less the power of human hatred,
  Sweeter far the Saviour's love.
Let me tell it to the needy,
  Far and wide Thy worth proclaim;
That my closing years may praise Thee—
  Glorify Thy blessed name.

Let me labor in Thy harvest
  More than ever in the past,
Reaping in what Thou hast planted,
  Till I dwell with Thee at last;
That before Thy throne eternal
  I may have some fruit to bring,
Not my work—the fruit of Calvary,
  All Thine own, my Lord and King.

WATCH AND PRAY

Christian, seek not yet repose,
  Cast thy dreams of ease away;
Thou art in the midst of foes;
  Watch and pray.

Gird thy heavenly armor on,
  Wear it ever night and day;
Near thee lurks the evil one;
  Watch and pray.

Hear the victors who o'ercame;
  Still they watch each warror's way;
All with one deep voice exclaim,
  "Watch and pray."

Charlotte Elliott

WOULD I BE CALLED A CHRISTIAN?

Would I be called a Christian,
If everybody knew
My secret thoughts and feelings,
And everything I do?
Oh, could they see the likeness
Of Christ in me each day?
Oh, could they hear Him speaking
In everything I say?

Would I be called a Christian,
If everybody could know
That I am found in places
Where Jesus would not go?
Oh, could they hear His echo
In every song I sing?
In eating, drinking, dressing,
Could they see Christ, my King?

Would I be called a Christian,
If judged by what I read,
By all my recreations,
And every thought and deed?
Could I be counted Christ-like,
As I now work and pray?
Unselfish, kind, forgiving
To others every day?

Mrs. J. F. Moser

GOD DOETH ALL THINGS WELL

I do not always know what lies before me,
  Or what of trial or test may be in store;
My steps are ordered, God will do the
  choosing,
  He knows the way I take—need I
  know more?
I do not know the reason for each testing;
  The lessons I must learn, I cannot tell,
Or why I'm led through valleys deep and
  lonely —
  I only know He doeth all things well.

If the path I walk seems steep and rugged,
  And I must labor long to reach the goal,
There's always One close by my side to
  help me;
  He brings sweet rest and comfort to
  my soul.
And from the pages of God's Book before
  me,
  He speaks the words that all my fears
  dispel,
And though I do not know the why nor
  wherefore,
  I can be sure He doeth all things well.

Then I will rest in Him and take fresh
  courage,
  And trust His promise not to leave me
  e'er —
New strength supplied to carry on the
  battle,
  New hope that I the victor's crown
  shall wear.
It is enough to be of God beloved,
  To have the Lord within my heart to
  dwell,
To have the peace that passeth under-
  standing,
  Content to know He doeth all things
  well.

FORGIVE ME WHEN I WHINE

Today upon a bus, I saw
  A lovely maid with golden hair;
I envied her — she seemed so gay —
  And oh, I wished I were so fair.
When suddenly she rose to leave,
  I saw her hobble down the aisle;
She had one foot and wore a crutch,
  But as she passed, a smile.
  Oh, God, forgive me when I whine;
  I have two feet — the world is mine.

And when I stopped to buy some sweets,
  The lad who served me had such charm.
He seemed to radiate good cheer
  His manner was so kind and warm.
I said, "It's nice to deal with you,
  Such courtesy I seldom find."
    He turned and said, "Oh, thank you,
    sir!"
  And I saw that he was blind.
  O, God, forgive me when I whine;
  I have two eyes — the world is mine.

Then, when walking down the street,
  I saw a child with eyes of blue.
He stood and watched the others play;
  It seemed he knew not what to do,
I stopped a moment, then I said:
  "Why don't you join the others, dear?"
He looked ahead without a word,
  And then I knew; He could not hear.
  Oh, God, forgive me when I whine;
  I have two ears — the world is mine.

With feet to take me where I'd go,
With eyes to see the sunset's glow,
With ears to hear what I should know:
  I'm blessed indeed. The world is mine:
  Oh, God, forgive me when I whine.

THE BLESSINGS OF SURRENDER

There's a sweetness in surrender,
  Counting not our will our own,
Then we always walk with Jesus,
  And the way is never lone.

For He talks to us so gently,
  His companionship is blest;
Oh, the calmness of surrender,
  Sweet, submissive, and at rest!

There's a safety in surrender,
  For our will oft leads astray,
But with it to Christ submitted,
  Never need we miss the way.

Then temptations lose their luring,
  For we're talking with the Lord,
And the world's vain call and clatter
  Fall upon our ears unheard.

There's a power in surrender,
  For the strength of God is ours,
Who has promised to deliver
  Out of all infernal powers.

Father, I would keep surrendered,
  I would walk alone with Thee,
In Thy presence I am happy,
  In Thy will my soul is free.

Free from care and strife and worry,
  Free from useless toil or pain;
Of my grief Thou makest glory,
  Of my labor greatest gain.
                    Mary J. Helphingtine

THE WORLD'S BIBLE

Christ has no hands but our hands
To do His work today;
He has no feet but our feet
To lead men in His way;
He has no tongues but our tongues
To tell men how He died;
He has no help but our help
To bring them to His side.

We are the only Bible
The careless world will read;
We are the sinner's Gospel,
We are the scoffer's creed;
We are the Lord's last message,
Given in deed and word;
What if the type is crooked?
What if the print is blurred?

What if our hands are busy
With work other than His?
What if our feet are walking
Where sin's allurement is?
What if our tongues are speaking
Of things His lips would spurn?
How can we hope to help Him
And hasten His return?
                    Annie Johnson Flint

BEING A CHRISTIAN

Being a Christian is living
As God would have us live.
Being a Christian is giving
All that we have to give.

Being a Christian is doing
Things that are pure and good.
Being a Christian is pursuing
All that we know we should.

Being a Christian is keeping
The Spirit of Christ within.
Being a Christian is seeking
The many lost souls to win.
                    Sunday School Banner

THINK IT OVER

I'll go where You want me to go, dear
Lord;
  Real service is what I desire;
I'll say what You want me to say, dear
Lord —
  But don't ask me to sing in the choir.

I'll say what You want me to say, dear
Lord;
  I like to see things come to pass;
But don't ask me to teach girls and boys,
  dear Lord —
  I'd rather just stay in my class.

I'll do what You want me to do, dear
Lord;
  I yearn for the Kingdom to thrive;
I'll give You my nickels and dimes, dear
Lord —
  But please don't ask me to tithe.

I'll go where You want me to go, dear
Lord;
  I'll say what You want me to say;
I'm busy just now with myself, dear
Lord —
  I'll help You some other day.

CHRIST'S BONDSERVANT

Make me a captive, Lord,
  And then I shall be free;
Force me to render up my sword,
  And I shall conqueror be.
I sink in life's alarms
  When by myself I stand;
Imprison me within Thine arms,
  And strong shall be my hand.

My heart is weak and poor
  Until it master find;
It has no spring of action sure —
  It varies with the wind;

It cannot freely move
  Till Thou hast wrought its chain;
Enslave it with Thy matchless love,
  And deathless it shall reign.

My will is not my own
  Till Thou hast made it Thine;
If it would reach a monarch's throne
  It must its crown resign:
It only stands unbent
  Amid the clashing strife,
When on Thy bosom it has lent
  And found in Thee its life.

George Matheson

WE WOULD SEE JESUS

To see the Lord the shepherds
  Were by the angel sent;
They spread the wondrous tidings
  With joy where'er they went,
The Baby in a manger
  Was God's own Son who came
To save from sin His people,
  For Jesus was His name.

Some earnest Greeks years after
  To His disciples came,
And said, "We would see Jesus,"
  For they had heard His fame.
They listened to His message,
  And saw His perfect grace;
They surely spread glad tidings
  Of Him in every place.

And, like the Greeks and shepherds,
  We would see Jesus, too,
And seek His grace to guide us
  In all we say and do.
So let us come and worship
  Our Saviour, Christ the Lord,
And, saved by His redemption,
  We'll spread the news abroad.

REPROOF

As children bring their broken toys,
  With tears, for us to mend,
I brought my broken dreams to God,
  Because He was my Friend.

But then, instead of leaving Him
  In peace, to work alone;
I hung around and tried to help
  With ways that were my own.

At last I snatched them back and cried,
  "How can You be so slow?"
"My child," He said, "what could I do?
  You never did let go!"

THE FATHER'S GOLD

A golden strand that weaves through
  tapestry
Goes sometimes, so it seems, so far astray
To pick up threads whose beauty we
  can't see,
Until the master weaver has His way.
The picture, woven then with artist's
  hand
Delights the eye with colors rich and
  bold;
The threads we thought so gray—each
  neutral strand —
Are interlaced with beauty, touched with
  gold.
Our Father weaves His plan in wisdom's
  way,
And some time, the whole pattern will
  unfold;
The treadle He will still, the shuttle stay,
Then Jesus Christ shall be revealed as
  gold —
The Shining Strand who interlaced our
  Grays
To lift, to hold and beautify always.

FOLLOW JESUS

I would follow Jesus
And know I may,
For I hear Him calling
And He shows me the way.

I would follow Jesus,
That my tongue may speak
Words which carry comfort
To the sad and the weak.

I would follow Jesus
As a child may do,
Be to all my comrades
Kind and pure and true.

I would follow Jesus —
This shall be my Prayer:
Dwell thou deep within me,
Prompt me everywhere.

THE POSTAGE STAMP LESSON

There was a little postage stamp
No bigger than your thumb;
But still it stuck right to the job
Until the work was done.

They licked it and they pounded it
'Til it would make you sick;
And the more it took a-lickin'
The better it would stick.

Let's all be like the postage stamp
In playing life's rough game;
And just keep on a-stickin'
Tho' we hang our heads in shame.

The stamp stuck to the letter
'Till it saw it safely through;
There's no one can do better
Let's keep sticking and be true.

SURPRISES

When you get to heaven
You will likely view
Many folk whose presence there
Will be a shock to you;

But keep it very quiet
And do not even stare;
Doubtless there'll be many
Surprised to see you there.

Christmas

HIS NAME AT THE TOP

I had the nicest Christmas list,
  The longest one in town,
Till Daddy looked at it and said,
  "You'll have to cut it down."

I knew that what he said was true
  Beyond the faintest doubt,
But was amazed to hear him say,
  "You've left your best Friend out."

And so I scanned my list again,
  And said, "Oh, that's not true!"
But Daddy said, "His name's not there,
  That Friend who died for you."

And then I clearly understood,
  'Twas Jesus that he meant;
For Him who should come first of all
  I hadn't planned a cent!

I'd made a Christmas birthday list,
  And left the Saviour out!
But, oh, it didn't take me long
  To change the list about.

And tho' I've had to drop some names
  Of folks I like a lot,
My Lord must have the most—because
  His name is at the top!

THE LIGHT NOW SHINETH

Angels from the long ago
  Told the old, old story
Of a Saviour come to earth
  From the realms of glory.

What a message they proclaimed,
  Angel hosts so bright,
As the shepherds on the hills
  Watched their flocks by night.

Unto you a child is born,
  Unto you is given,
Emmanuel, the Son of God,
  The Lord Himself, from heaven.

See the gift of God's own love,
  Go ye to the manger,
He, who left His home above,
  Is to you no stranger.

Ye who sit in darkness, look,
  For the Light now shineth,
He will great deliverance give you
  From the chains that bindeth.

Love eternal, never dying,
  Ransoms from the grave,
Souls in conflict, burdened, sighing,
  Jesus came to save.

CRADLE AND THRONE

Earth gave Thee a cradle, O Christ, and
a cross,
Hard roads for Thy journey, reviling and
loss;
Earth gave Thee Thy wounding, Thy
shroud, and Thy tomb,
But earth gave no welcome and earth
gave no home.

Oh, Wronged One, return to the land
Thou hast left,
The land that is desolate, lone, and bereft;
The world is a chaos of comfortless woes;
Men's wisdom has failed them, no help
they propose,

Thou art the one hope, Lord, oh, lend
us Thine aid
And save Thy creation—the world Thou
hast made.
A new earth shall greet Thee, a new world
shall sing
The greatness and glories of Jesus its
King.

Earth that once gave Thee its scorning
and shame,
Its thorns and its scourging, shall yet hail
Thy name,
The earth, once rebellious, allegiance
shall own,
Shall give Thee a scepter, a crown, and
a throne.

A CHILD IS BORN

That holy night when stars shone bright,
Our hearts beat high with joy;
A baby's birth upon the earth,
Held hope without alloy.

Shepherds in fright made hasty flight,
And sped to the stable bed;
They kneeled to pray where the baby lay
And worshiped the hallowed head.

Three kings so wise beheld the skies,
They saw a moving star;
It guided them to Bethlehem,
From distant lands afar.

O blessed morn a child is born,
In a manger on the hay;
Let angels sing, hosannas ring,
A King has come today.

JOY TO THE WORLD

Joy, great joy, was the message
Told to shepherds in the field.
An angel brought the tidings,
The good news from heav'n revealed.
In haste they sped to find Him,
Born a Babe, before Him kneeled.
They knew He was the Saviour.
He was God in flesh concealed.
To all the heartsick, sad ones
In this whole wide world today.
To the worn and weary pilgrims
Filled with fear, distrust, dismay,
Our Christ sounds the same message
As the angels did that day.
On Calv'ry's cross He suffered
To bring joy to all for aye.

The world is filled with sorrow
Caused by unbelief and sin,
Rejection of this Saviour
Who alone can cleanse within.
Some day He'll smite the nations,
Too late then His grace to win.
It's now He offers pardon
And gives joy where grief has been.

Christ's Coming

SAFELY HOME

I am home in heaven, dear ones;
  All's so happy, all so bright!
There's perfect joy and beauty
  In this everlasting light.

All the pain and grief are over,
  Every restless tossing passed;
I am now at peace forever,
  Safely home in heaven at last.

Did you wonder I so calmly
  Trod the Valley of the Shade?
Oh! but Jesus' love illumined
  Every dark and fearful glade.

And He came Himself to meet me
  On that way so hard to tread;
And with Jesus' arm to lean on,
  Could I have one doubt or dread?

Then you must not grieve so sorely,
  For I love you dearly still;
Try to look beyond earth's shadows,
  Pray to trust our Father's will.

There is work still waiting for you,
  So you must not idle stand;
Do your work while life remaineth —
  You shall rest in Jesus' land.

When that work is all completed,
  He will gently call you home;
Oh, the rapture of the meeting!
  Oh, the joy to see you come!

WHEN WILL HE COME?

Perhaps He will come at the dawning
  Of a beautiful summer day,
When the birds and flowers are
    awakening
  To welcome the sun's first ray,
And the eastern sky will brighten
  With the light of the dawn's caress
And herald the swift arising
  Of the "Sun of Righteousness."

Perhaps He will come at the evening
  When, weary of toil and care,
We rest and watch as the darkness
  Creeps o'er the landscape fair,
And behind, the stars in their beauty
  Shine forth from their depths afar,
But their radiance dims in the glory
  Of the "Bright and Morning Star."

Perhaps He will come at midnight,
  When earth and its dwellers sleep.
When over the mountains and valleys
  Broods a silence vast and deep,
And the trump of the great archangel
  Shall awaken the slumberers there,
And His saints will be caught up together
  To meet the Lord in the air.

But whether at dawn or evening,
  At midnight or sultry noon,
And whether awake or sleeping,
  And the time be distant or soon,
May I live so that I shall be ready
  With joy my Saviour to meet,
And feel no alarm at His coming,
  But hasten His heralds to greet.

CHRIST IS COMING

In the glow of early morning,
  In the solemn hush of night;
Down from heaven's open portals,
  Steals a messenger of light,
Whisp'ring sweetly to my spirit
  While the hosts of heaven sing;
This the wondrous thrilling story:
  Christ is coming — Christ the King.

Oft methinks I hear His footsteps,
  Stealing down the paths of time;
And the future, dark with shadows,
  Brightens with this hope sublime.
Sound the soul-inspiring anthem;
  Angel hosts, your harps attune;
Earth's long night is almost over,
  Christ is coming — coming soon.

Long we've waited, blest Redeemer,
  Waited for the first bright ray
Of the morn when sin and sorrow
  At Thy presence flee away;
But our vigil's nearly over;
  Hope of heaven oh, priceless morn;
In the east the glow appearing,
  Christ is coming — coming soon.
                    W. Macomber

THE COMING AND THE APPEARING

Lamb of God, Thy faithful promise
  Says, "Behold, I quickly come,"
And our hearts, to Thine responsive,
  Cry, "Come, Lord, and take us home."
Oh, the rapture that awaits us
  When we meet Thee in the air,
And with Thee ascend in triumph,
  All Thy deepest joys to share.

Lamb of God, when Thou in glory
  Shalt to this sad earth return,

All Thy foes shall quake before Thee,
  All who now despise Thee mourn;
Then shall we, at Thine appearing,
  With Thee in Thy kingdom reign,
Thine the praise, and Thine the glory,
  Lamb of God for sinners slain.

PERHAPS TODAY

Perhaps today the clouds will part
    asunder,
  Reveal a glory brighter than the sun,
And we shall view with transport, joy and
    wonder,
  The hope of earth and heaven's beloved
    One.

Perhaps today the world's last taunt shall
    grieve us,
  And Satan, foiled, his final dart shall
    cast,
And all our flesh's frailties shall leave us,
  And disappointment evermore be past.

Perhaps today from weary beds of
    anguish
  God's suffering saints shall breathe
    their final sigh,
In glory rise, no more on earth to
    languish,
  To meet their great Deliv'rer in the
    sky.

Perhaps today the trump of God re-
    sounding,
  Shall wake the sleepers from their beds
    of clay,
And we with them our longed-for Lord
    surrounding,
  Shall see His glorious face — perhaps
    today!

30

HOPE OF OUR HEARTS

Hope of our hearts, O Lord! appear:
    Thou glorious Star of day,
Shine forth, and chase the dreary night,
    With all our fears, away!

Strangers on earth, we wait for Thee:
    Oh! leave the Father's throne;
Come with the shout of victory, Lord,
    And claim us for Thine own!

Oh! bid the bright archangel now
    The trump of God prepare,
To call Thy saints—the quick, the dead—
    To meet Thee in the air.

No resting-place we seek on earth,
    No loveliness we see;
Our eye is on the royal crown
    Prepared for us and Thee.

But, dearest Lord, however bright
    That crown of joy above,
What is it to the brighter hope
    Of dwelling in Thy love?

What to the joy—the deeper joy,
    Unmingled, pure, and free—
Of union with our Living Head,
    Of fellowship with Thee?

This joy e'en now on earth is ours:
    But only, Lord, above,
Our hearts, without a pang, shall know
    The fullness of Thy love.

There, near Thy heart, upon the throne,
    Thy ransomed bride shall see
What grace was in the bleeding Lamb
    Who died to make her free.

Sir Edward Denny

GOING HOME WITH JESUS

I am going home with Jesus
    As the days go passing by,
For we're having sweet communion —
    To His heart He draws me nigh —
And He tells me He will keep me
    If I trust Him all the way,
And be humble, meek and lowly,
    And His Holy Word obey.

O I'm going home with Jesus —
    Precious truth it is to me —
And it makes my heart so happy
    When I think of what shall be
My reward for being faithful
    As a servant on the earth —
Life eternal and no trouble,
    Peace and everlasting mirth!

I am going home with Jesus —
    Soon we'll pass the pearly gates —
And I'll occupy a mansion
    That I know for me awaits,
Where I'll dwell with shining angels
    And my loved ones sweet and fair,
Who have passed me on life's journey
    And are waiting for me there.

When I reach my home in heaven
    Where I'll live for evermore,
I will sing and shout God's praises
    With the saints who've gone before,
Where we'll have no times of sadness
    And no seasons of distress,
But in holy love and worship
    We shall have the sweetest rest.

Walter E. Isenhour

The Church

THE FAITHFUL FEW

In every church, in every clime,
  When there's some work to do;
It very likely will be done
  By just a faithful few.

While many folks will help to sing
  And some of them will talk,
When it comes down to doing things
  A lot of them will balk.

"We can't do this, we can't do that,
  Excuse us, please — this time;
We'd be so glad to help you out,
  But it's not in our line."

So when the leader casts about
  To find someone who'll "do,"
Although he's done it oft before,
  He asks the Faithful Few.

Of course, they're very busy, too,
  And always hard at work;
But well he knows they'll not refuse
  Nor any duty shirk.

They never stop to make excuse,
  But promptly try to do
The very very best they can
  To smooth the way for you.

God bless, I pray, the faithful few,
  And may their tribe increase —
They must be very precious to
  The blessed Prince of Peace.

Chester E. Shuler

GOD IS THERE

When your Christian duty calls you
  To the sick and to the sad,
And you go to take some sunshine
  And to make somebody glad,
You may have the sweet assurance
  As you breathe an earnest prayer,
That the place where you are going
  God the Father will be there.

If you want to help the outcast
  Find the pathway to the goal,
Or the wretched, poor lost sinner
  Seek salvation for his soul;
Or someone who seems quite hopeless,
  And for whom there's little care,
Go and look for such dear people
  And our God will meet you there.

In the prisons of our country
  Men are found behind the bars,
Who have fallen from their manhood,
  In whose lives are many scars,
So they need someone to help them,
  Who some Christian love may share,
Then go forth and help the prisoner
  And you'll find the Saviour there.

Or if you are burdened heavy
  With the cares of friends and home,
Or temptations, tests and trials
  Where you live and where you roam,
Don't surrender faith and courage,
  Neither quit the place of prayer,
For the God of earth and heaven
  Always meets His children there.

Walter E. Isenhour

IT'S YOU

If you want to work in the kind of a
  church
  Like the kind of a church you like,
You needn't slip your clothes in a grip
  And start on a long, long hike.

You'll only find what you left behind.
  For there's nothing that's really new;
It's a knock at yourself when you knock
  your church;
  It isn't your church, it's you.

Real churches aren't made by men afraid
  Lest somebody else goes ahead;
When everyone works and nobody shirks,
  You can raise a church from the dead.

And if while you make your personal
  stake,
  Your neighbor can make one too,
Your church will be what you want to see,
  It isn't your church, it's you.

L. A. McDonald

GREAT CHURCHES

Great churches aren't built of stone and
  steel,
  Of mortar, brick and sand;
They rise from human hearts that feel
  And love and understand.

Their greatest treasures are not kept
  In guarded banks or vaults,
But in the will that never slept
  Until it cured its faults.

Great churches don't happen; they are
  built
  By people large and small
Who press their fortunes to the hilt,
  Respond to duty's call.

I WOULD NOT ASK

I would not ask Thee why
  My path should be
Through strange and stony ways —
  Thou leadest me!

I would not ask Thee how
  Loss worketh gain,
Knowing that some day soon —
  All shall be plain.

My heart would never doubt
  Thy love and care,
However heavy seems
  The cross I bear.

Nor would I, Father, ask
  My lot to choose,
Lest seeking selfish ease
  Thy best I lose.

Grace E. Troy

CONCERNING THEM THAT ARE ASLEEP

Alas! too well we know our loss,
  Nor hope again our joy to touch,
Until the stream of death we cross.
  He smiled: "There is no such!"

Yet our beloved seem so far,
  The while we yearn to feel them near,
Albeit with Thee we trust they are.
  He smiled: "And I am here!"

Dear Lord, how shall we know that they
  Still walk unseen with us and Thee,
Nor sleep, nor wander far away?
  He smiled: "Abide in me."

R. W. Raymond

33

NOAH'S CARPENTERS

Many hundred years ago,
 They ventured to remark,
That Noah had some carpenters
 To help him build the Ark.
But sad to say on that last day,
 When Noah entered in,
Those carpenters were left outside
 And perished in their sin.

How sad to think they may have helped
 To build the Ark so great!
Yet still they heeded not God's Word,
 And awful was their fate.
To-day the same sad state exists
 Among the sons of men;
They help to build the so-called church,
 Who are not born again.

They stay behind for sacrament,
 They work, they sing, they pray;
Yet never have accepted Christ,
 The Life, the Truth, the Way.
Another Judgment Day will come,
 As sure as came the flood,
And only those will be secure.
 Who shelter 'neath Christ's blood.

HOW CAN YOU?

How can you comfort the suffering
 If you've not known sickness or pain?
How can you spur on the fighter
 When you've never known battle's
  strain?

How can you soothe the impatient
 If you've not been tested in stress?
How can you lift the discouraged
 When you've never known weariness?

How can you strengthen the traveler
 Unless heavy burdens you've borne?
How can you cheer the sorrowing heart
 If your heart has never been torn?

God does not revel in trouble,
 But this thing I've been made to see—
I can't be used to help others
 If trials are foreign to me.

I must endure pain and sorrow,
 Encounter defeat and distress
To teach me compassion and mercy
 For souls He is waiting to bless.
 Maxine Stevens

THE EVER-LIVING CHURCH

Come, let us join our friends above
 That have obtained the prize,
And on the eagle wings of love
 To joy celestial rise.
Let all the saints terrestrial sing
 With those to Glory gone;
For all the servants of our King
 In earth and heaven are one.

One company we dwell in Him —
 One Church above, beneath —
Though now divided by the stream,
 The narrow stream of death.
One army of the living God,
 To His command we bow;
Part of His host hath crossed the flood,
 And part is crossing now.

Our old companions in distress
 We haste again to see,
And eager long for our release
 And full felicity.
E'en now by faith we join our hands
 With those that went before,
And greet the Blood-besprinkled bands
 On the eternal shore.
 Charles Wesley

DO YOU JUST BELONG?

Are you an active member,
  The kind that would be missed?
Or are you just contented
  That your name is on the list?
Do you attend the meetings
  And mingle with the crowd?
Or do you stay at home
  And crab both long and loud?

Do you take an active part
  To help the church along
Or are you satisfied to be
  The kind that just belong?
Do you ever go to visit
  A member that is sick,

Or leave the work for just a few
  And talk about the clique?

There's quite a program scheduled
  That means success if done,
And it can be accomplished
  With the help of everyone.
So attend the meetings regularly,
  And help with hand and heart —
Don't be just a member,
  But take an active part.

Think this over, member:
  Are we right or are we wrong?
Are you an active member?
  Or do you just belong?

Comfort — Sorrow

THE GOD OF COMFORT

I have been through the valley of
  weeping,
  The valley of sorrow and pain;
But the God of all comfort was with me,
  At hand to uphold and sustain.

As the earth needs the clouds and the
  sunshine
  Our souls need both sorrow and joy,
So He places us oft in the furnace,
  The dross from the gold to destroy.

When He leads through some valley of
  trouble
  His omnipotent hand we can trace;
For the trials and sorrows He sends us
  Are part of His lessons of grace.

Oft we shrink from the purging and
  pruning,

Forgetting the husbandman knows
That the deeper the cutting and paring
  The richer the cluster that grows.

Well He knows that affliction is needed
  He has a wise purpose in view;
And in the dark valley He whispers,
  "Hereafter thou shalt know what I do."

As we travel through life's shadowed
  valley,
  Fresh springs of His love ever rise,
And we learn that our sorrow and losses
  Are blessings just sent in disguise.

So we'll follow wherever He leads us,
  Let the path be dreary or bright,
For we've proved that our God can give
  comfort,
  Our God can give songs in the night.

COMFORTING LINES

Can it be possible no words shall welcome
    Our coming feet?
How will it look, that face that we have
    cherished,
    When next we meet?
Will it be changed, so glorified and
    saintly
    That we shall know it not?
Will there be nothing that will say, "I
    love thee,
    And I have not forgot"?

Oh! faithless heart, the same loved face
    transfigured
    Shall meet thee there,
Less sad, less wistful, in immortal beauty
    Divinely fair.
The mortal veil, washed pure with many
    weepings,
    Is rent away,
And the great soul that sat within its
    prison
    Hath found the day.

In the clear morning of that other
    country,
    In paradise,
With the same face that we have loved
    and cherished
    She shall arise!
Let us be patient, we who mourn, with
    weeping,
    Some vanished face,
The Lord has taken, but to add more
    beauty
    And a diviner grace.

And we shall find once more, beyond
    earth's sorrows
    Beyond these skies,
In the fair city of the "sure foundations,"
    Those heavenly eyes.

With the same welcome, shining through
    their sweetness,
    That met us here;
Eyes, from whose beauty God has
    banished weeping
    And wiped away the tear.

HE NEVER WILL FORGET

Jesus never will forget me,
    When I'm young, or when I'm old.
With His precious blood He bought me;
    So, you see, to Him I'm sold.

He could not forget His loved ones,
    Who to Him are very dear;
Resting in His loving bosom
    I have not a single fear.

In His hands my name is written,
    In His heart He thinks of me;
And He'll soon come back to take me
    Where with Him I'll always be.
                M. G. H

THE MASTER WEAVER

When gray threads mar life's pattern
And seem so out of line,
Trust the Master Weaver
Who planned the whole design;

For in life's choicest patterns
Some dark threads must appear
To make the rose threads fairer,
The gold more bright and clear.

The pattern may seem intricate
And hard to understand,
But trust the Master Weaver
And His steady, guiding Hand.

CONSOLATION

There is never a day so dreary
  But God can make it bright,
And unto the soul that trusts Him,
  He giveth songs in the night,
There is never a path so hidden,
  But God can lead the way,
If we seek for the Spirit's guidance
  And patiently wait and pray.

There is never a cross so heavy
  But the nail-scarred hands are there
Outstretched in tender compassion
  The burden to help us bear.
There is never a heart so broken,
  But the loving Lord can heal,
The heart that was pierced on Calvary
  Doth still for His loved ones feel.

There is never a life so darkened,
  So helpless and unblessed,
But may be filled with the light of God
  And enter His promised rest.
There is never a sin or sorrow,
  There is never a care or loss,
But that we may bring to Jesus
  And leave at the foot of the cross.

OUR ROCK

If life's pleasures cheer thee,
  Give them not thy heart,
Lest the gifts ensnare thee
  From thy God to part;
His praises speak, His favor seek,
  Fix there thy hope's foundation,
Love Him, and He shall ever be
  The Rock of thy salvation.

If sorrow e'er befall thee,
  Painful though it be,
Let not fear appall thee;
  To thy Saviour flee;

He, ever near, thy prayer will hear,
  And calm thy perturbation;
The waves of woe shall ne'er o'erflow
  The Rock of thy salvation.

Death shall never harm thee,
  Shrink not from his blow,
For thy God shall arm thee
  And victory bestow;
For death shall bring to thee no sting,
  The grave no desolation;
'Tis gain to die with Jesus nigh —
  The Rock of thy salvation.

Francis Scott Key

TRIALS

I Peter 1:7; Romans 8:28

When trials press and foes increase
  And daily strain finds no release;
Give me the strength and will to stay
  When I would rather run away.

When things seem going all criss-cross
  And waiting seems an added loss;
Give me the patience, Lord, to wait
  When I would rather force the gate.

When Satan comes with subtle power
  To make me doubt Thy love each hour;
Give me the grace to trust Thy care
  When self would plunge me in despair.

The God of all the universe,
  Who from my soul removed the curse,
Is daily watching over me
  And will through all eternity.

So faith looks up and takes the stand
  That love divine the whole has planned,
And step by step will guide my way
  Till dawns at last eternal day.

Grace E. Troy

37

SOMETIME, SOMEWHERE

Unanswered yet? the prayer your lips
have pleaded
In agony of heart these many years.
Does faith · begin to fail? Is hope
departing?
And think you all in vain those falling
tears?
Say not the Father hath nor heard your
prayer;
You shall have your desire sometime,
somewhere.

Unanswered yet? though when you first
presented
This one petition at the Father's throne
It seems you could not wait the time of
asking
So urgent was your heart to make it
known.
Though years have passed since then, do
not despair;
The Lord will answer you sometime,
somewhere.

Unanswered yet? nay, do not say un-
granted.
Perhaps your part is not yet wholly done.
The work began when first your prayer
was uttered
And God will finish what He has begun.
If you will keep the incense burning there
His glory you shall see sometime, some-
where.

Unanswered yet? faith cannot be
unanswered.
Her feet are firmly planted on the Rock;
Amid the wildest storm, she stands
undaunted;
Nor quails before the loudest thunder-
shock.

She knows Omnipotence has heard her
prayer
And cries, "It shall be done sometime,
somewhere!"

THE NAME OF JESUS

How sweet the name of Jesus sounds
  In a believer's ear;
It soothes his sorrows, heals his wounds,
  And drives away his fear.

It makes the wounded spirit whole,
  And calms the troubled breast;
'Tis manna to the hungry soul,
  And to the weary rest.

John Newton

WITH THEE

In darkest hours, in nights so drear,
When heart is faint and full of fear,
Just lift your voice to God and pray;
And darkest night will turn to day.

He promised to protect and keep;
To never slumber, never sleep.
Though worn and helpless you may be,
The promise comes, "I am with thee."

Through waters deep, He'll walk with
  you
And through the fiery trials too.
He is your God, be not dismayed.
Be sure your trust in Him is stayed.

He'll give you strength and hold your
  hand.
In storm and strife, He'll help you stand.
Supported by His arm alone,
Peace will be yours, the greatest known.

Cora M. Pinkham

HE KNOWS THE WAY

I know not where my steps may lead
  In days to come;
But He, who for my sins did bleed,
  Will guide me home.

And though the road be rough and steep,
  I'll have no dread;
For He, who for my sins did weep,
  Walks on ahead.

Though valleys dark and mountains high
  May bar my way;
Through Him, who on the cross did die,
  I'll win the day.

And at life's end, my journey o'er
  I'll see the face
Of Him who journeyed on before —
  Saved by His grace.

CASTING ALL YOUR CARE UPON HIM

When from a world of tumult we retreat,
  To commune with the Lord in secret
  prayer,
We often bring our burdens to His feet
  Who bids us cast on Him our every
  care.

We do, but find that we have failed to
  leave them there;
  So when again the busy world we meet,
We lack that peace of God so truly sweet,
  Which comes of telling God our wants
  in prayer.

Oh, let us "roll our burdens on the Lord"
  And leave them there, although our
  way be dim,
His peace our lot, our care consign'd to
  Him.

His grace accepts and now sustains
our load.

WHAT GOD HATH PROMISED

God hath not promised
  Skies always blue,
Flower-strewn pathways
  All our lives through;
God hath not promised
  Sun without rain,
Joy without sorrow,
  Peace without pain.

God hath not promised
  We shall not know
Toil and temptation,
  Trouble and woe;
He hath not told us
  We shall not bear
Many a burden,
  Many a care.

God hath not promised
  Smooth roads and wide,
Swift, easy travel,
  Needing no guide;
Never a mountain,
  Rocky and steep,
Never a river
  Turgid and deep.

But God *hath* promised
  Strength for the day,
Rest for the labor,
  Light for the way,
Grace for the trials,
  Help from above,
Unfailing sympathy,
  Undying love.

              Annie Johnson Flint

MY HIDING PLACE

Thou art my Hiding Place,
  Lord of my life;
In Thee I rest,
  Free from all strife.

Thou art my Fortress safe,
  Lord of my heart;
Thou art e'er near,
  Grace to impart.

Thou art my All in All,
  Lord of my soul;
O Guiding Star,
  Thou art my Goal!

For this I thank Thee, Lord:
  Through Thy sweet grace,
I have found Thee —
  My Hiding Place!
                    Kathryn T. Bowsher

RULES FOR DAILY LIFE

Begin the day with God;
  Kneel down to Him in prayer;
Lift up thy heart to His abode
  And seek His love to share.

Open the Book of God,
  And read a portion there;
That it may hallow all thy thoughts
  And sweeten all thy care.

Go through the day with God,
  Whate'er thy work may be.
Where'er thou art — at home, abroad,
  He still is near to thee.

Converse in mind with God;
  Thy spirit heavenward raise;
Acknowledge every good bestowed,
  And offer grateful praise.

Conclude the day with God;
  Thy sins to Him confess.
Trust in the Lord's atoning blood,
  And plead His righteousness.

Lie down at night with God,
  Who gives His servants sleep;
And when thou tread'st the vale of death
  He will thee guard and keep.

COMPANIONSHIP

No distant Lord have I,
  Loving afar to be;
Made flesh for me, He cannot rest
  Unless He rests in me.

Brother in joy and pain,
  Bone of my bone was He,
Now—intimacy closer still,
  He dwells Himself in me.

I need not journey far
  This dearest Friend to see;
Companionship is always mine,
  He makes His home with me.

I envy not the Twelve,
  Nearer to me is He;
The life He once lived here on earth
  He lives again in me.

Ascended now to God,
  My witness there to be,
His witness here am I because
  His Spirit dwells in me.

O glorious Son of God,
  Incarnate Deity,
I shall forever be with Thee
  Because Thou art with me.
                    Maltbie D. Babcock

40

SUBMISSION IN AFFLICTION

Affliction is a stormy deep,
  Where wave resounds to wave:
Though o'er my head the billows roll
  I know the Lord can save.

The hand that now withholds my joys
  Can soon restore my peace;
And He who bade the tempest rise
  Can bid that tempest cease.

Here will I rest, and build my hope,
  Nor murmur at His rod;
He's more than all the world to me —
  My Health, my Life, my God!

NOT CHANGED, BUT GLORIFIED

Not changed but glorified! Oh, beauteous
    language
  For those who weep,
Mourning the loss of some dear face
    departed,
  Fallen asleep.
Hushed into silence, never more to
    comfort
  The hearts of men,
Gone, like the sunshine of another
    country,
  Beyond our ken.

O dearest dead, we saw thy white soul
    shining
  Behind the face,
Bring with the beauty and celestial glory
  Of an immortal grace.
What wonder that we stumble, faint and
    weeping
  And sick with fears,
Since thou hast left us — all alone with
    sorrow
  And blind with tears?

NOT I, BUT GOD

I cannot, but God can;
  Oh, balm for all my care!
The burden that I drop
  His hand will lift and bear.
Though eagle pinions tire,
  I walk where once I ran,
This is my strength, to know
  I cannot, but God can.

I know not, but God knows;
  Oh, blessed rest from fear!
All my unfolding days
  To Him are plain and clear.
Each anxious, puzzled "Why?"
  From doubt or dread that grows,
Finds answer in this thought:
  I know not, but He knows.

Annie Johnson Flint

THE BIRDS OF THE AIR

No storehouse nor barn have we,
  The fluttering birds of the air;
No voice to make known our wants,
  With hunger our only prayer.
Yet God feedeth us day by day,
  As the light of the morn comes round,
And never without His leave
  Shall one of us fall to the ground.

O Saviour! I hear Thy voice
  In these happy birds of the air,
Who sow not, gather, nor reap,
  Yet lack not a Father's care.
They trust to a guiding Hand,
  Which feedeth them day by day:
What want they with storehouse or barn?
  And are we not better than they?

Hollis Freeman

41

SECURITY

More secure is no one ever
Than the loved ones of the Saviour;
Not yon star, on high abiding,
Nor the bird in home-nest hiding.

God His own doth tend and nourish,
In His holy courts they flourish;
Like a father kind He spares them,
In His loving arms He bears them.

Neither life nor death can ever
From the Lord His children sever;
For His love and deep compassion
Comfort them in tribulation.

Little flock, to joy then yield thee!
Jacob's God will ever shield thee;
Rest secure with this Defender,
At His will all foes surrender.

What He takes or what He gives us
Shows the Father's love so precious;
We may trust His purpose wholly —
'Tis His children's welfare solely.

Lina Sandell

THROUGH THE WATERS

When thou passest through the waters,
Deep the waves may be and cold,
But Jehovah is our refuge,
And His promise is our hold;
For the Lord Himself hath said it,
He, the faithful God and true:
When thou comest to the waters,
Thou shalt not go down, but through.

Seas of sorrow, seas of trial,
Bitterest anguish, fiercest pain,
Rolling surges of temptation
Sweeping over heart and brain —
They shall never overflow us,
For we know His word is true;
All His waves and all His billows,
He will lead us safely through.

Threatening breakers of destruction,
Doubt's insidious undertow,
Shall not sink us, shall not drag us
Out to ocean depths of woe;
For His promise shall sustain us,
Praise the Lord, whose Word is true!
We shall not go down, or under,
For He saith, "Thou passest through."

Annie Johnson Flint

Communion-Consecration

WHAT IS THAT IN THINE HAND?

In Moses' hand 'twas but a rod
That showed the Father's power;
With David 'twas a sling that made
Him God's man of the hour.

It wasn't silver, neither gold
That Peter had to give;

And Dorcas but a needle had
Whereby to sew and live.

All by His power, our mighty God's,
His great omnipotence;
We see His will and work well done
Yoked with our impotence.

Eva Gray

THIS BLESSED CHRIST
OF CALVARY

He gives to me His wondrous grace,
And shows to me His tender face;
Prepares me for a heavenly place,
This blessed Christ of Calvary!

O broken heart, let Him come in!
He'll save you from your every sin;
O'er every foe the vict'ry win,
This blessed Christ of Calvary!

Just come to Him this very hour,
He brings to you His saving pow'r;
With real joys your soul will show'r,
This blessed Christ of Calvary!

Someday He's coming then for me;
From death to ever set me free;
I'll live with Him for eternity,
This blessed Christ of Calvary!

"THIS DO IN REMEMBRANCE
OF ME"

(Luke 22:19)

I came from far for thee,
    In love the long way down;
I left My throne for thee.
    I wore a thorn-set crown.
All this I did for thee!
Wilt thou *remember Me?*

I bore thy sins for thee.
    Wept tears of deepest woe:
I bore God's wrath for thee
    To make thee white as snow.
Could love do more for thee?
Wilt thou *remember Me?*

I tasted death for thee.
    Bore shame thy sins had wrought.
My life laid down for thee

To thee Life endless brought.
What is My death to thee?
Dost thou *remember Me?*

I gave Myself for thee
    My all was freely given
Thy Bread of Life to be.
    Thy Manna come from heaven.
All this am I to thee.
Eat and *remember Me.*

I drank thy cup for thee.
    Thy cup of pain and tears.
My hands have filled for thee
    My cup of sinless joy.
Of blessing full and free.
Drink and remember Me.

DELIVER ME

From prayer that asks that I may be
Sheltered from winds that beat on Thee,
From fearing when I should aspire,
From faltering when I should climb
    higher,
From silken self, O Captain, free
Thy soldier who would follow Thee.

From subtle love of softening things,
From easy choices, weakenings
(Not thus are spirits fortified,
Not this way went the Crucified),
From all that dims Thy Calvary,
O Lamb of God, deliver me.

Give me the love that leads the way,
The faith that nothing can dismay,
The hope no disappointments tire,
The passion that will burn like fire;
Let me not sink to be a clod;
Make me Thy fuel, Flame of God.

Amy Carmichael

43

I MET THE MASTER

I had walked life's way with an easy
   tread,
Had followed where comforts and
   pleasures led,
Until one day in a quiet place
I met the Master face to face.

With station and rank and wealth for my
   goal,
Much thought for my body but none for
   my soul,
I had entered to win in life's mad race,
When I met the Master face to face.

I met Him and knew Him and blushed
   to see,
That His eyes full of sorrow were fixed
   on me;
And I faltered and fell at His feet that
   day,
While my castles melted and vanished
   away.

Melted and vanished and in their place
Naught else did I see but the Master's
   face.
And I cried aloud, "Oh, make me meet
To follow the steps of Thy wounded feet."

My thought is now for souls of men,
I have lost my life to find it again,
E'er since one day in a quiet place
I met the Master face to face.

A HEART THAT WEEPS

Oh, for a heart that weeps o'er souls,
   Weeps with a love in anguish born!
Oh, for a broken, contrite heart,
   A heart for sinners rent and torn!

Oh, for the pangs of Calv'ry's death,
   In fellowship with Thee, my Lord!
Oh, for the death that lives in life,
   And bleeds for those who spurn Thy
   Word!

Naught have I sought of blessing, Lord,
   Save that which brings lost souls to
   Thee;
All else is vain, nor dare I boast —
   This, Lord, I crave, be this my plea.

Have Thou Thy way whate'er the cost,
   In death I live, in life I die;
Thy way, not mine, dear Lord, I pray,
   Souls, precious souls, my ceaseless cry.
                 Oswald J. Smith

DISCERNING THE LORD'S BODY

Let me discern by living faith
   The Christ who died for me,
Behold His precious body crushed
   And bleeding on the Tree.

Then let me still discern by faith
   That dear ascended Lord,
His body in the glory heights,
   Yet here in power and Word.

And as I show His precious death
   Until my Lord doth come
Let me discern the coming Christ
   To take me to my Home.

Thus I shall never fail to see
   In all His fullness blest
The Christ who died and rose for me,
   And in whose Word I rest.

And when in glory from the skies
   I see Him as He is,
My body shall be glorified
   And shall be made like His.
            Carrie Judd Montgomery

THE GOSPEL ACCORDING TO YOU

If none but you in the world today
Had tried to live the Christlike way,
Could the rest of the world look close at
    you
And find the path that is strait and true?

If none but you in the world so wide
Had found the Christ for his daily guide,
Would the things you do and the things
    you say
Lead others to live in His blessed way?

Ah, friends of the Christ, in the world
    today
Are many who watch you upon your way,
And look to the things you say and do
To measure the Christian standard true:

Men read and admire the Gospel of Christ
With its love so unfailing and true,
But what do they say and what do they
    think
Of the gospel according to you?

You are writing each day a letter to men
Take care that the writing is true;
'Tis the only gospel that some men will
    read,
That gospel according to you.

TRUE WISDOM

True wisdom is in leaning
    On Jesus Christ, our Lord;
True wisdom is in trusting
    His own life-giving word;
True wisdom is in living
    Near Jesus every day;
True wisdom is in walking
    Where He shall lead the way.

THE BREAD OF LIFE

Break thou the bread of life,
    Dear Lord, to me,
As thou dids't break the loaves
    Beside the sea;
Beyond the sacred page
    I seek Thee, Lord;
My spirit thirsts for Thee,
    O Living Word.
Bless Thou the truth, dear Lord,
    To me, to me,
As Thou didst bless the loaves
    By Galilee;
Then shall all bondage cease,
    All fetters fall;
And I shall find my peace,
    My all in all.

Mary A. Lathbury

ADORATION

I love my God, but with no love of mine,
    For I have none to give;
I love Thee, Lord, but all the love is
    Thine
    For by Thy love I live.
I am as nothing, and rejoice to be
Emptied and lost and swallowed up in
    Thee.

Thou, Lord, alone art all Thy children
    need.
    And there is none beside;
From Thee the streams of blessedness
    proceed,
    In Thee the blest abide —
Fountain of life and all-abounding grace,
Our source, our center, and our dwelling
    place.

Madame Guyon

45

THE RIDICULOUS OPTIMIST

There was once a man who smiled
  Because the day was bright,
  Because he slept at night,
  Because God gave him sight
To gaze upon his child;
  Because his little one,
  Could leap and laugh and run;
  Because the distant sun
Smiled on the earth he smiled.

He smiled because the sky
  Was high above his head,
  Because the rose was red,
  Because the past was dead!
He never wondered why
  The Lord had blundered so
  That all things have to go
  The wrong way, here below
The over-arching sky.

He toiled, and still was glad
  Because the air was free,
  Because he loved, and she
  That claimed his love and he
Shared all the joys they had!
  Because the grasses grew,
  Because the sweet winds blew,
  Because that he could hew
And hammer, he was glad.

THE SECRET

I met God in the morning
  When the day was at its best,
And His presence came like sunrise,
  Like a glory in my breast.

All day long the presence lingered,
  All day long He stayed with me,
And we sailed in perfect calmness
  O'er a very troubled sea.

Other ships were blown and battered,
  Other ships were sore distressed,
But the winds that seemed to drive them
  Brought to us a peace and rest!

Then I thought of other mornings,
  With a keen remorse of mind,
When I too had loosed the moorings
  With the Presence left behind.

So I think I know the secret,
  Learned from many a troubled way;
You must seek Him in the morning
  If you want Him through the day.

  Ralph S. Cushman

THE MASTER'S CALL

Have you heard the Master's call?
Will you go forsaking all?
Millions still in sin and shame
Ne'er have heard the Saviour's name.

Some may give and some may pray,
But for you He calls today —
Will you answer: "Here am I,"
Or must Jesus pass you by?

Have you heard their bitter cry?
Can you bear to see them die,
Thousands who in darkest night,
Never yet have seen the light?

Soon 'twill be too late to go .
And your love for Jesus show.
Oh, then quickly haste away —
Tarry not another day!

What if you refuse to go?
Someone then will never know
Of the Saviour kind and true,
And the blame will rest on you.

Will you then forsaking all,
Gladly heed the Master's call:
Answer quickly, "Lord, send me!
To the lands beyond the sea"?

  Oswald J. Smith

ONLY ONE LIFE

Only one life to live here,
Only one message to share,
Only one thought for tomorrow —
The meeting in the air!

Only a few more trials,
Only a few more cares,
Then, oh then, we'll rejoice in
The meeting in the air!

Only a passion for lost ones,
Only a heart filled with care,
Only a life — lived for Jesus, then
The meeting in the air!

Only the blood-bought sinners,
Only the saved will be there
To behold the face of Jesus, in
The meeting in the air!

Gladys M. Bowman

HAVE I DONE MY BEST FOR JESUS?

I wonder, have I giv'n my best to Jesus
Who died upon the cruel tree?
To think of His great sacrifice at Calv'ry,
I know my Lord expects the best from me.

How many are the lost that I have lifted?
How many are the chained I've helped to free?
I wonder, have I done my best for Jesus,
When He has done so much for me?

The hours that I have wasted are so many,
The hours I've spent for Christ so few.
Because of all my lack of love for Jesus,
I wonder if His heart is breaking too?

I wonder have I cared enough for others,
Or have I let them die alone?
I might have helped a wand'rer to the Saviour;
The seed of precious life I might have sown.

No longer will I stay within the valley,
I'll climb to mountain heights above;
The world is dying now for the want of someone
To tell them of the Saviour's matchless love.

Ensign Edwin Young

SAVED, BUT —

I am saved, but is self buried?
Is my one, my only aim,
Just to honor Christ my Saviour,
Just to glorify His name?

I am saved, but is my home life
What the Lord would have it be?
Is it seen in every action,
Jesus has control of me?

I am saved, but am I doing
Everything that I can do,
That the dying souls around me,
May be brought to Jesus, too?

I am saved, but could I gladly,
Lord, leave all and follow Thee?
If Thou callest can I answer,
"Here am I, send me, send me"?

THE HIGHER CALLING

We may not work a miracle
   In any given place,
But we can be a miracle
   Of God's redeeming grace.
The call to work a miracle
   May be for one short day:
The gift to be a miracle
   Shall never pass away.

             W. M. Czamanske

OPEN MY EYES

Open my eyes, that I may see
   This one and that one needing Thee:
Hearts that are dumb, unsatisfied;
   Lives that are dark, for whom Christ
      died.

Open my eyes in sympathy
   Clear into man's deep soul to see;
Wise with Thy wisdom to discern.
   And with Thy heart of love to yearn.

Open my eyes in power, I pray,
   Give me the strength to speak today,
Someone to bring, dear Lord, to Thee;
   Use me, O Lord, use even me.

            Betty Scott Stam

THE PROMISE

I've tried in vain, day after day
To work and live in such a way

That my resolves would all be kept
But I have failed and often wept.

And then I learned Christ died for me
And so I knelt at Calvary

Hoping tumultuous thoughts would cease,
That I might find some precious peace.

It did not come in startling ways;
But I have found salvation pays.

The still, small voice whispered to me,
"I'll make you what you want to be."

            Mary B. Fowler

Desire

ONE THING I OF THE LORD DESIRE

One thing I of the Lord desire,
   For all my way hath miry been:
Be it by water or by fire,
   O make me clean!

If clearer vision Thou impart,
   Grateful and glad my soul shall be;
But yet to have a purer heart
   Is more to me.

Yea, only as the heart is clean
   May larger vision yet be mine,

For mirrored in its depths are seen
   The things divine.

I watch to shun the miry way,
   And stanch the spring of guilty
      thought:
But, watch and wrestle as I may,
   Pure I am not.

So wash Thou me without, within;
   Or purge with fire, if that must be;
No matter how, if only sin
   Die out in me.

MY HEART'S DESIRE

Come, Spirit of Thy Holy Love,
  Into this poor life of mine,
Make Thou in me Thy dwelling place
  That I'll be wholly Thine.

Help me to live for others, Lord,
  That they will plainly see

The beauty of Thy Holy Life,
  Reflected, Lord, in me.

Then when I stand before Thee, Lord
  And lay my trophies down,
Wilt Thou receive them, Lord of grace,
  And give to me a crown?

Determination

IT COULDN'T BE DONE

Somebody said that it couldn't be done
But with a chuckle he replied
That "maybe it couldn't" but he would be
  the one
Who wouldn't say until he tried,
So he buckled right in, with a trace of
  a grin
On his face. If he worried, he hid it.
He started to sing as he tackled the thing
That couldn't be done, and he did it.

Somebody scoffed, "Oh you'll never do
  that
At least no one has ever done it";
But he took off his coat and he took off
  his hat,
And the first thing we knew he'd begun it.
With the lift of his chin and a bit of a
  grin,
Without any doubting or "quiddit,"
He started to sing as he tackled the thing
That couldn't be done, and he did it.

There are thousands to tell you it cannot
  be done,
There are thousands to prophesy failure;

There are thousands to point out to you,
  one by one,
The dangers that wait to assail you;
But just buckle in with a bit of grin
Just take off your coat and go to it;
Just start in to sing as you tackle the
  thing
That "cannot be done" and you'll do it.

HIS BEST

God has His best things for the few
Who dare to stand the test,
God has His second choice for those
Who will not take His best.
And others make the highest choice,
But when by trials pressed,
They shrink, they yield, they shun the
  cross,
And so they lose His best.
I want in this short life of mine
As much as can be pressed
Of service true for God and man
Help me to be Thy best.
I want among the victor-throng
To have my name confessed,
And hear the Master say at last
"Well done! you did your best."

49

DON'T QUIT

When things go wrong as they sometimes
  will,
When the road you're trudging seems all
  uphill,
When funds are low and debts are high,
And you want to smile, but have to sigh,
When care is pressing you down a bit—
Rest if you must, but don't quit.

Life is queer with its twists and turns,
As every one of us sometimes learns;
And many a fellow turns about
When he might have won, had he stuck
  it out.
Don't give up though the pace seems
  slow
You may succeed with another blow.

Often the goal is nearer than
It seems to a faint and faltering man;
Often the struggler has given up
When he might have captured the victor's
  cup;
And he learned too late when the night
  came down,
How close he was to winning the crown.

Success is failure turned inside out
The silver tint of the clouds of doubt,
You never can tell how close you are,
It may be near, when it seems afar;
So stick to the fight when you're hardest
  hit
It's when things seem worst that you
  mustn't quit.

JUST KEEP ON KEEPIN' ON

If the day looks kinder gloomy,
  An' your chances kinder slim!

If the situation's puzzlin'
  An' the prospect's awful grim,

An' perplexities keep pressin'
  Till all hope is nearly gone,

Jus' bristle up an' grit your teeth
  An' keep on keepin' on.

Fumin' never wins a fight,
  An' frettin' never pays

There ain't no good of broodin' in
  These pessimistic ways —

Smile just kinder cheerfully
  When hope is nearly gone,

An' bristle up an' grit your teeth,
  An' keep on keepin' on.

There ain't no use in growlin'
  An' grumblin' all the time,

When music's ringing everywhere
  An' everything's a rhyme —

Jus' keep on smilin' cheerfully,
  If hope is nearly gone,

An' bristle up an' grit your teeth,
  And keep on keepin' on.

KEEP YOUR GRIT

Hang on! Cling on! No matter what
they say.
Push on! Sing on! Things will come
your way.
Sitting down and whining never helps a
bit;
Best way to get there is by keeping up
your grit.

Don't give up hoping when the ship goes
down,
Grab a spar or something — just refuse
to drown.

Don't think you're dying because you're
hit.
Smile in face of danger and hang on to
your grit.

Folks die too easy — they sort of fade
away,
Make a little error, and give up in
dismay.
Kind of man that's needed is the man of
ready wit,
To laugh at pain and trouble and keep
his grit.

The Devil

THE DEVIL

Men don't believe in a devil now,
As their fathers used to do;
They've forced the door of the broadest
creed
To let his majesty through;
There isn't a print of his cloven foot
Or a fiery dart from his bow
To be found in earth and air today,
For the world has voted so.

But who is mixing the fatal draught
That palsies heart and brain,
And loads the earth of each passing year
With ten hundred thousand slain?

Who blights the bloom of the land today
With the fiery breath of hell?
If the devil isn't and never was
Won't somebody rise and tell?

Won't somebody step to the front forth-
with,
And make his bow and show
How the frauds and the crimes of the day
spring up?
For surely we want to know.
The devil was fairly voted out,
And of course the devil is gone;
But simple people would like to know
Who carries his business on?

51

Discipleship

DISCIPLESHIP

"He saith unto them, Follow Me" (Matthew 4:19).

Matthew left his place of toil
  And Christ as Lord confessed,
Zacchaeus left his wayside tree
  And entertained his guest;
And Mary left her household tasks
  To hear her Master's voice,
While fishers' left their boats and nets,
  And followed Christ from choice;
A woman left her water-pots
  To spread good news abroad;
Then gladly will I leave my all
  To follow Christ my Lord.

C. O. Bales

MY BOOK OF LIFE

I closed another chapter
  In my book of life today,
And paused for meditation
  As I laid the book away.

I thought of smudgy pages
  Where the record was not clear,
And dreary lines of trouble
  Clouded o'er by doubt and fear.

It's now too late to alter
  Any script that's dried and set;
The story's far from perfect,
  But it's vain to stew and fret.

I asked the Lord to pardon
  The mistakes that mar the book,

And give me grace and courage
  By a hopeful, Christ-ward look.

So now, there lies before me
  A new chapter clean and white.
And I hope to write its pages
  So the plot will turn out right.

I trust the final chapters
  Will the Master's plan reveal,
And weave the many fragments
  To depict a life that's real.

Frances Humphrey

THE COST

You say it will cost much to follow,
  But what will it cost to refuse?
You may gain the world and its glories,
  But what if your soul you thus lose?

You say He may call you to follow
  Leaving all that to you is so dear
Yea, even to give your own life blood
  That souls still in darkness may hear.

If you would thus follow the Master
  On the altar all things must be laid
He gave His own life as a ransom,
  His blood your redemption has paid.

Be sure you count the cost rightly
  Putting value where value should be
If you put Jesus first and His glory
  All things will be added to thee.

Flora L. Osgood

HEARTSEARCH

Am I emptied, Lord, of self?
Search this sinful heart of mine;
Bring the hidden secrets out
To the view of love divine.

Probe my motives, thoughts, and plans,
Attitudes, and loves, and will;
Until I see, as Thou dost see,
Self poured out, so Thou canst fill.

Fill with love — thus Thou canst bless
Others through this house of clay
Yielded, fruitful, in Thy will,
Following in Thy perfect way.

Evelyn K. Gibson

CHRIST IN YOU

Has someone seen Christ in you today?
Christian, look at your heart, I pray.
The little things you have done or said—
Did they accord with the way you
    prayed?
Have your thoughts been pure and words
    been kind?
Have you sought to have the Saviour's
    mind?
The world with a criticizing view
Has watched — but did it see Christ
    in you?

Has someone seen Christ in you today?
Christian, look at your life, I pray;
There are aching hearts and blighted
    souls
Being lost in sin's destructive shoals.
And perhaps of Christ, their only view
May be what of Him they see in you.
Will they see enough to bring hope and
    cheer?
Look at your light, does it shine out
    clear?

I KNOW

I know not what my health will be,
    But this I know full well —
Sufficient it will be for me
    To do my Lord's work well.

I know not what that work will be,
    But this I fully know:
That I'll have opportunity
    For tasks that God doth show.

I know not where God's choice may be
    For me my years to spend,
But this I know — He'll be with me
    Until those years shall end.

Verda Group

I TURN TO JESUS

I cannot turn from Jesus,
    He means so much to me;
My sins He has forgiven,
    His grace has set me free.
I journey on to heaven
    With Him, my Friend, my guide,
For He will never leave me
    No matter what betide.

I turn from all that grieves Him
    And seek to do His will;
He carries all my burdens,
    I know He loves me still.
Oh, precious Lord and Saviour,
    How dear He is to me!
I glory in His presence
    And long His face to see.

I turn to Him in sorrow
    When tempted and opprest,
I find Him all He promised,
    My Strength, my Joy, my Rest.
His grace is all sufficient
    However dark my way;
I worship and adore Him
    And praise Him night and day.

Oswald J. Smith

53

Discouragement

HE GIVETH MORE GRACE

He giveth more grace when the burdens
　　grow greater,
　　He sendeth more strength when the
　　labors increase;
To added affliction He addeth His mercy,
　　To multiplied trials, His multiplied
　　peace.

When we have exhausted our store of
　　endurance;
　　When our strength has failed e'er the
　　day is half done;
When we reach the end of our hoarded
　　resources
　　Our Father's full giving is only begun.

His love has no limit, His grace has no
　　measure,
　　His power no boundary known unto
　　men;
For out of His infinite riches in Jesus
　　He giveth and giveth, and giveth again.
Annie Johnson Flint

DON'T

Don't get discouraged when you hear
　　What people say about you;
Don't get the blues and drop a tear
　　Because they chance to doubt you.

Don't go around with troubled brow,
　　O'erlooking all life's' beauty;
The folks that talk will suffer more
　　Than you, so do your duty.

Don't fret and fume and wish them ill,
　　Their lives hold little pleasure;
Send back a message of good will —
　　'Twill serve to heap your measure.

Don't be discouraged, for the world
　　Will always criticize you;
Earth's dearest treasure is the few
　　True friends who love and prize you.

MISTAKES

Erasers are such handy things
　　On pencils, there's no doubt.
A few quick rubs, the wrong words go,
　　Mistakes are soon rubbed out.

But errors of a different sort
　　That cannot be erased,
Are often spilled from someone's lips,
　　And cannot be replaced.

And with each thoughtless spoken word,
　　Sharp as a leopard's tooth,
The harm we do is just as great,
　　As some widespread untruth.

But with these careless spoken words,
　　Erasers play no part.
The mark we leave, by word or deed,
　　Cuts deep in someone's heart .
George W. Swarberg

WHEN THINGS GO WRONG

Do not spend your time in fretting;
Spend it, rather, in forgetting
　　Little things that wound you so.
　　Do not let the whole world know
That you'd rather sit a-grieving
When you might be out relieving
　　Pain and care. Rise up, be true!
　　Just find something good to do.

When your days are full of sighing,
Don't give up, but keep on trying
　　Some good cause to help along,
　　You will soon forget the wrong
That the dismal days are bringing,
If you time your work to singing.
　　When your skies are dark in hue,
　　Just find something good to do.

When your life seems full of trouble,
Pain and care will always double,
　　If you talk about your woes;
　　Also will your skies disclose
Brighter tints upon the morrow,
When the lessons taught by sorrow
　　Help instead of hinder you.
　　Just find something good to do.

Spend no time in dull repining;
Everywhere the sun is shining.
　　And the future ways are bright,
　　If we truly see aright.
Life is what we make it, truly,
And 'twill seldom go unruly
　　If the right course we pursue —
　　Just find something good to do.

DISCOURAGED

We mustn't get discouraged at the things
　　which people say
We mustn't get depressed if things refuse
　　to go our way
We must be just like Joshua with faith
　　to battle on
To just "be of good courage" with the
　　Lord to lean upon.

Things sometime seem to cloud the way,
　　but after comes the sun
We see the cloud's significance when all
　　the storm is done.
Our wish would often not be right, but
　　harmful and unjust
The thing that's best will come, if we in
　　God will put our trust.

Lucille Stanaback

Easter

NOT THERE

Oh, the anguish of Mary!
Her grief and despair
When she came to the tomb
And the Lord was not there!
As she silently stood
With her balm and her myrrh,
And His winding-sheet only
Was waiting for her.

Oh, the blackness of death!
Life's utter despair
Had she not come to the tomb,
And the Lord had been there
Lying wrapped in the shroud,
With the balm and the myrrh,
And no risen Redeemer
Had waited for her.

THE CROSS AND THE TOMB

"He died," saith the cross, "my very
      name
   Was a hated thing and a word of
      shame;
But since Christ hung on my arms out-
      spread,
   With nails in His hands and thorns on
      His head,

They do but measure — set high, flung
      wide —
   The measureless love of the Crucified."
"He rose," said the tomb, "I was dark and
      drear,
   And the sound of my name wove a
      spell of fear;

But the Lord of Life in my depths hath
      lain
   To break Death's power and rend his
      chain;
And a light streams forth from my open
      door,
   For the Lord is risen; He dies no
      more."

   Annie Johnson Flint

THE SEPULCHER

The Man had died on the cross,
   And they laid Him in the tomb;
The Living Stone in the stone,
   The Rock in the rock-hewn room;
They left Him alone with Death,
   And sealed the stone at the door;
They made the sepulcher secure,
   And set their watch before.

"Lest his friends should steal him away,
   And say that he rose," they said.
But Life escaped from Death,
   And the God-man rose from the dead.

The skeptical minds of men
   Still think the sepulcher sure,
But Christ had said, "I will arise,"
   And the counsels of God endure.

Still His disciples go
   To carry the wondrous word:
"The Lord is risen indeed!
   We know — we have seen and heard."
And the tomb men think so sure,
   With the seal of their scorn on the door,
The place where the Lord once lay,
   Is empty forevermore.

   Annie Johnson Flint

HIS LIFE IS OURS

We must not, in our hurried lives,
   Forget the cross whereby
Christ Jesus died that we might live
   And find Him ever nigh.
Yes, Jesus died in agony
   Such as we cannot know,
For on His precious head were laid
   Our sin and shame and woe!

Between the earth and sky He hung
   That He might reconcile
Our hearts to God and give us life,
   Not only for awhile,
But for eternity! What great,
   What selfless sacrifice,
That we may resurrection know
   Since He has paid the price!

The cross has crumbled now, and lies
   As dust within the ground,
But Christ will live forevermore,
   And grace will e'er abound!
No need have we to fear, for He
   Has conquered, for us all,
Sin, shame, and death; His life is ours
   Whatever may befall!

   Dorothy Conant Stroud

HE LIVES! HE LIVES TO BLESS!

He lives! He lives! He lives to bless
 Each heart that welcomes Him!
He lives as truly now as when
 In shadows cool and dim
He walked along the garden path
 All wet with morning dew,
Where sleepy birds were wakening
 And fragrant lilies grew.

He lives! He lives! He lives today
 As truly as of yore,
When angels rolled away the stone
 And opened wide the door.
He lives! He lives! O earth rejoice!
 For Jesus lives today,
And, oh, His blessed presence can
 Each doubt and fear allay.

He lives! He lives! Oh, can we doubt
 That living presence when
The life He promised He would give
 Dwells in the hearts of men?
Then, O rejoice! The Saviour lives!
 Rejoice and own Him King!

Then all of heaven's blessedness
Into your heart He'll bring!
Dorothy Conant Stroud

EASTER, DAY OF CHRIST ETERNAL

In the inn they had no room.
One who loved Him loaned his tomb.
Death could not hold Him nor its prey,
There in earth but grave-clothes lay!

From the death He died for sin,
Came our Conqueror forth to win!
On the third day rose "The King!"
Of His triumph Christians sing.

Hallelujah! Join the chorus,
Magnify our Saviour Jesus!
Tell the world His blood has power,
Shout aloud His grace this hour!

Easter, day of Christ eternal!
Satan conquered in His world.
Time of praise and prayer and glory
Matchless Christ, Oh, wondrous story.
Maurice Moore

Examination

INFLUENCE

I spoke a word
And no one heard:
I wrote a word
And no one cared:
But after a half a score of years
It blossomed in a fragrant deed.
Preachers and teachers all are we,
Sowers of seed unconsciously.
Our hearts are beyond our ken,
Yet all we give may come again
With usury of joy and pain;
We never know
To what one little word may grow
See to it, then, that all your seed
Be such as bring forth noble deed.
John Oxenham

DO IT NOW

He was going to be all that a mortal
  should be — Tomorrow.

No one should be kinder or braver than he
  — Tomorrow.

A friend who was troubled and weary he
  knew,
Who'd be glad of a lift, and who needed
  it, too;
On him he would call and see what he
  could do — Tomorrow.

Each morning he stacked up the letters
  he'd write — Tomorrow.
And thought of the folks he would fill
  with delight — Tomorrow.

It was too bad, indeed, he was busy today,
And hadn't a minute to stop on his way;
More time he would have to give others,
  he'd say — Tomorrow.

The greatest of workers this man would
  have been — Tomorrow.

The world would have known him had he
  ever seen — Tomorrow.

But the fact is he died, and he faded from
  view,
And all that he left, when living was
  through,
Was a mountain of things he intended to
  do — Tomorrow.

REFLECTION

One day I looked at myself,
  At the self that Christ can see;
I saw the person I am today,
  And the one I ought to be.
I saw how little I really pray,
  How little I really do;
I saw the influence of my life,
  How little of it was true!
I saw the bundle of faults and fears
  I ought to lay on the shelf;

I had given a little bit to God —
  But I hadn't given myself.
I came from seeing myself,
  With my mind made up to be
The sort of person that Christ can use,
  With a heart He may always see.

AT THE PLACE OF THE SEA

*"By the greatness of thine arm they shall be still . . .
till thy people pass over, O Lord"—Exodus 15:16.*

Have you come to the Red Sea place in
  your life,
  Where, in spite of all you can do,
  There is no way out, there is no back,
  There is no other way but—through?
Then wait on the Lord with a trust serene
  Till the night of your fear is gone;
He will send the wind, He will heap the
  floods,
  When He says to your soul, "Go on."

And His hand will lead you through —
  clear through—
  Ere the watery walls roll down,
No foe can reach you, no wave can touch,
  No mightiest sea can drown;
The tossing billows may rear their crests,
  Their foam at your feet may break,
But over their bed you shall walk dry
  shod
  In the path your Lord will make.

In the morning watch, 'neath the lifted
  cloud,
  You shall see but the Lord alone,
When He leads you on from the place of
  the sea
  To land that you have not known;
And your fears shall pass as your foes
  have, passed,
  You shall be no more afraid;
You shall sing His praise in a better
  place,
  A place that His hand has made.

Annie Johnson Flint

WHAT I SEE IN ME

I have so many faults myself
    I seldom ever see
A defect in another's life
    But what I see in me,
I make so many rash mistakes
    I feel condemned to find
A bit of fault in everyone
    When I'm so far behind.

I used to censure everyone;
    I was a Pharisee,
Until quite unexpectedly
    I got a glimpse of me,
I tried to justify myself
    And frame some alibi;
But here I stood, caught by myself
    And I to me won't lie.

And now whenever I'm inclined
    Some other's judge to be,
I always go and take a look
    At him whom I call me,
I find it is a splendid thing —
    Just try it and you'll see —
To keep from criticizing folk,
    Let each "I" look at "Me."

LET ME LOOK AT ME

I know I have a lot of faults
    I never even see,
But my neighbor knows about them,
    For he is watching me!

I try to walk exemplary,
    Obeying God's commands,
But never see the little sins
    My neighbor understands!

I readily can see his faults,
    They stand out sharp and strong,
And am amazed he cannot see
    What is so clearly wrong.

And then I am convicted
    As the Spirit whispers low,
"If you would truly judge yourself,
    No judgment you would know."

I humbly ask God's pardon,
    And beg Him search within
And show me all the little things
    I do not see as sin.

That when I judge my neighbor.
    As all his faults I see,
I'll turn my eyes away from him,
    And look instead at me.
                    Bessie June Martin

MY NEED

I need a strength to keep me true
And straight in every thing I do;
I need a power to keep me strong
When I am tempted to do wrong;
I need a grace to keep me pure
When passion tries its deadly lure;
I need a love to keep me sweet
When hardness and mistrust I meet;
I need an arm to be my stay
When dark with trouble grows my way;
And nought on earth can these afford
But all is found in Christ my Lord.

A COMPARISON

We fear to judge a watermelon
By the exterior view,
We plug it for a peep inside,
To see if it will do.

Now man is like the melon
That's sold down on the mart;
We cannot rightly judge him
Unless we see his heart.

But since we haven't vision
This job to undertake,
We'd better leave it up to God,
And save a sad mistake.

Evolution

THREE MONKEYS

Three monkeys once dining in a cocoanut
tree
Were discussing some things they had
heard true to be,
"What do you think? now listen you two,
Here, monkeys, is something that cannot
be true,
That humans descended from our pure
race.
Why, it's simply shocking — a terrible
disgrace.

"Who ever heard of a monkey deserting
his wife?
Leave a baby starve and ruin its life?
And have you ever known of a mother
monk
To leave her darling, with a stranger to
bunk?
Their babies are handed from one to
another
And scarce ever know the love of a
mother.

"And I've never known a monkey so
selfish to be
As to build a big fence around the cocoanut tree
So other monkeys can't get a wee taste,
But would let all the cocoanuts here go
to waste.
Why, if I'd put a fence around this cocoanut tree,
Starvation would force you to steal from
me.

"And here is another thing a monkey
won't do,
Seek a bootlegger's shanty and get in
a stew,
Carouse and go on a whoopee, disgracing
his life,
Then reel madly home and beat up his
wife
They call this all a pleasure and make a
big fuss,
They've descended from something, but
not from us."

Faith

TRUST HIM

Trust Him when dark doubts assail thee,
Trust Him when thy strength is small
Trust Him when to simply trust Him
Seems the hardest thing of all.

Trust Him, He is ever faithful,
Trust Him, for His will is best,

Trust Him, for the heart of Jesus
Is the only place of rest.

Trust Him through cloud or sunshine
All thy cares upon Him cast
Till the storms of life are over,
And the trusting days are past.

PERFECT LOVE

Perfect love the Father giveth,
　Full of grace so rich and free,
Like the rain or dew of morning
　Falling now on you and me.

Perfect love is born in Jesus,
　Naught of self can victory gain,
Till we find it all in Jesus
　All our efforts prove but vain.

Perfect love will never falter
　Perfect love will never fear,
And when the days are dark and stormy
　Perfect love will always cheer.

Perfect love will never slander,
　Friend or foe where e'er they go;
But will raise a fallen brother,
　And will take his seat below.

Perfect love that long will suffer,
　Never murmur or complain,
Never ask her own, or covet
　Others' wealth, or earthly fame.

Perfect love is meek and lowly,
　Perfect love is rich and free,
Perfect love is Jesus only,
　Come to dwell in you and me.

LIGHT AND LOVE,
HOPE AND FAITH

Light is made to shine in darkness,
　Let us, in this world of woe,
Shine as luminaries; brighten
　Dismal pathways as we go.

Love is sent to rout the hatred
　Of a sad and sin-cursed earth;
Let us love and lift in kindness,
　Through our Saviour, give it mirth.

Hope is born to cheer the faint heart,
　'Tis the bright and morning star
To the weary, ladened pilgrim;
　As he, trusting, looks afar.

Faith, a ladder, still is reaching
　From beyond the beck'ning skies;
Charts the course of every Christian,
　Leads us on to paradise.

Eva Gray

THAT'S FAITH

Looking away from my sin and my
　shame,
Looking away from my sorrow and pain,
Looking to Jesus, the Lamb that was
　slain —
　That's faith.

Looking away from my knowledge and
　pride,
Looking to Jesus my Shepherd and
　Guide,
Looking to Jesus and Him crucified —
　That's faith.

Looking away from my gain or my loss,
Looking away from the world and its
　dross,
Looking to Jesus on Calvary's cross —
　That's faith.

Looking away from my faith or its lack,
Looking to Jesus, whose Word is not
　slack,
Looking to Jesus and turning not back—
　That's faith.

S. N. Leitner

FEATHERED FAITH

Said the sparrow to the robin,
"I would surely like to know
What makes these busy humans
Rush about and worry so!"

Said the robin to the sparrow,
"I don't know unless it be
They have no Heavenly Father
To care for them like you and me."

THE GOD IN WHOM WE TRUST

Not in works or vain endeavors,
    To fulfill a broken law,
Not in empty forms and fashions
    From which some their comfort draw:
But in God, who ever liveth
    And who ever loves to bless
All who in His mercy trusteth,
    All who do His Christ confess.

Faith in God who loves the sinner,
    Trust in Christ who died to save,
Simply taking what He offers,
    Just accepting what He gave.
Brings at once the glad assurance

Of forgiveness by His grace,
Full acceptance in His favor,
    And among His sons a place.

HAVE FAITH IN GOD

When inclined to be discouraged
    And all hope seems to depart,
Don't forget that Jesus liveth
    And still has you on His heart.

When your load seems hard to carry
    And the burden no one shares,
Though the world seems not to pity
    Just remember, Jesus cares.

When thou passest through the waters
    And no earthly help you see,
Do not lose your faith in God, for
    He has said, "I'll be with thee."

So, dear heart, fear not, take courage,
    For the Word of God is true.
Jesus said, "I'll never leave thee,
    But will guide while passing through."
                              Joe Budzynski

Father

SERVICE SUPREME

A careful man I ought to be;
A little fellow follows me.
I do not dare to go astray
For fear he'll go the selfsame way.

I cannot once escape his eyes;
Whate'er he sees me do he tries.
Like me he says he's going to be,
The little chap who follows me.

He thinks that I am good and fine,
Believes in every word of mine.
The base in me he must not see,
That little chap who follows me.

I must remember as I go
Thro' summer's sun and winter's snow,
I'm building for years to be —
That little chap who follows me.

DOES DADDY GO?

Daddy had a little boy,
  His soul was white as snow
He never went to Bible school,
  'Cause Daddy wouldn't go.

He never heard the Word of God
  That thrills the childish mind
While other children went to class,
  This child was left behind.

As he grew from babe to youth,
  Dad saw to his dismay,
A soul that once was snowy white,
  Became a dingy gray.

Realizing that his son was lost,
  Dad tried to win him back;
But now the soul that once was white,
  Had turned an ugly black.

Dad even started back to church
  And Bible study too;
He begged the preacher, "Isn't there
  A thing that you can do?"

The preacher tried, failed, and said,
  "We're just too far behind;
I tried to tell you years ago,
  But you would pay no mind."

And so another soul was lost,
  That once was white as snow;
Bible school would have helped
  But Daddy wouldn't go.

A FATHER SPEAKS

Father in heaven, make me wise,
So that my gaze may never meet
A question in my children's eyes.
God, keep me always kind and sweet,
And patient, too, before their need;

Let each vexation know its place,
Let gentleness be all my creed,
Let laughter live upon my face!
A Father's day is very long,
There are so many things to do!
But never let me lose my song
Before the harvest day is through.

DAD'S GREATEST JOB

I may never be as clever as my neighbor
  down the street,
I may never be as wealthy as some other
  men I meet;
I may never have the glory that some
  other men have had,
But I've got to be successful as a little
  fellow's dad.
There are certain dreams I cherish that
  I'd like to see come true,
There are things I would accomplish ere
  my working time is through;
But the task my heart is set on is to guide
  a little lad
And to make myself successful as that
  little fellow's dad.
It is that one job I dream of; it's the task
  I think of most;
If I'd fail that growing youngster I'd
  have nothing else to boast;
For though wealth and fame I'd gather,
  all my future would be sad,
If I'd failed to be successful as that little
  fellow's dad.
I may never get earth's glory; I may
  never gather gold;
Men may count me as failure when my
  business life is told;
But if he who follows after is a Christian,
  I'll be glad —
For I'll know I've been successful as a
  little fellow's dad.

TO ANY DADDY

There are little eyes upon you, and
they're watching night and day;
There are little ears that quickly take in
every word you say;
There are little hands all so eager to do
everything you do,
And a little boy who's dreaming of the
day he'll be like you.

You're the little fellow's idol, you're the
wisest of wise;
In his little mind about you no suspicions
ever rise;
He believes in you devoutly, holds that
all you say and do
He will say and do in your way too when
he's grown up like you.

There's a wide-eyed little fellow who
believes you're always right,
And his ears are always open and he
watches day and night.

You are setting an example every day in
all that you do,
For the little boy who's waiting to grow
up to be like you.

DEAR OLD DAD

So often we praise our mothers here and
merit all their ways.
We so ignore the fact that Dad he, too,
deserves some praise.
Who strives to earn the daily bread? To
keep all healthy — glad?
Isn't he that gets so little praise And
that is dear old Dad.

To praise our mothers, that is good (This
they may deserve)
Yet why so slack in praising Dad and
keep in reserve?
Let's measure their equalities — give
merits, praise, when due.
Start pinning laurels on your Dad, He's
done a lot for you.

Eva Gilbert Shaver

Future

INVOCATION FOR THE NEW YEAR

God give you faith this coming year!
The faith that will not fail in keenest test;
That trusts and sings in midst of fire and
storm;
And dares rely upon His Word and rest.

God give you hope this coming year!
The hope that through the darkness sees
afar
The purifying hope that fondly waits

The rising of the Bright and Morning
Star.

God give you Love this coming year!
His own great love that burns out for the
lost;
That intercedes, and waits, and suffers
long
That never fails, nor stops to count the
cost.

Margaret D. Armstrong

THIS TOO WILL PASS AWAY

When some great sorrow, like a mighty
river,
Flows through your life with peace des-
troying power,
And dearest things are swept from sight
forever,
Say to your aching heart each trying
hour,
"This too, this too, will pass away."

When ceaseless toil has hushed your song
of gladness
And you have grown almost too tired to
pray,
Let this truth banish from your heart its
sadness,
And ease the burden of each trying day:
"This too, this too, will pass away."

When fortune smiles, and full of mirth
and pleasure
The days are flitting by without a care,
Lest you should rest with only earthly
treasure,
Let these few words their fullest import
bear:
"This too, this too, will pass away."

When earnest labor brings you fame
and glory,
And all earth's noblest ones upon you
smile,
Remember that life's longest, grandest
story
Fills but a moment in earth's little while:
"This too, this too, will pass away."

Thank God that earthly things are not
forever,
Thank God, eternal life is free today;
That joy and peace and gladness reigneth
ever,

And bliss supreme shall never, never pass
away.

THE BEST CHOICE

He knows, He loves, He cares,
 Nothing this truth can dim,
He gives the very best to those
 Who leave the choice with Him.

GOD'S PAY

Who does God's work will get God's pay,
However long may be the day.
He does not pay as others pay,
In gold, or land, or raiment gay,
In goods that perish or decay;
But God"s high wisdom knows the way,
And this is sure, let come what may —
Who does God's work will get God's pay.

TOMORROW

In His hands I leave tomorrow;
For my Heavenly Father knows
What is needed for my future;
When it comes He will disclose
Ways and means I could not reckon,
As His all-providing power
Brings to pass the right solution,
All sufficient for each hour.

As I meet with firm assurance
What the present now requires,
I am given strength and purpose,
So I ask that my desires
May be righteous, just, and kindly,
Measured by His love, I pray:
In His hands I leave tomorrow
As I walk with Him today.

Della Adams Leitner

65

WE'LL MEET AGAIN

We'll meet again the loved ones gone
before us —
In that bright realm the land of light and
love;
It may be that e'en now they're watching
o'er us,
And longing for the time we'll meet
above.

We'll meet again of that we may be
certain,
In that bright home so wondrous and so
fair,
Whose glories, veiled to us as by a
curtain,
Through God's redeeming grace we are
to share.

We'll meet where neither sadness nor
sorrows
Shall for one moment rob the heart of joy;
Where there shall be no dark uncertain
morrows,
Or aught whatever to the bliss destroy.

Ah, yes, we'll meet again in that bright
glory;
How wondrous it will be to talk things
o'er,
And to begin a fresh, but never-ending
story
Of life which shall endure forevermore.

J. Danson Smith

GOD IS IN EVERY TOMORROW

God is in every tomorrow,
Therefore I live for today,
Certain of finding at sunrise,
Guidance and strength for the day;
Power for each moment of weakness;
Hope for each moment of pain,

Comfort for every sorrow,
Sunshine and joy after rain.

God is in every tomorrow,
Planning for you and for me;
E'en in the dark will I follow,
Trust where my eyes cannot see.
Stilled by His promise of blessing,
Soothed by the touch of His hand,
Confident in His protection,
Knowing my life-path is planned.

God is in every tomorrow,
Life with its changes may come,
He is behind and before me,
While in the distance shines Home!
Home where no thoughts of tomorrow
Ever can shadow my brow,
Home in the presence of Jesus,
Through all eternity now!

OUR TIMES ARE IN HIS HANDS

Have you committed all to God?
Then be assured He'll do the rest,
If He the sparrow's fall doth note,
He'll surely hover o'er thy nest.

He clothes the lily of the field
Each blade of grass receives His dew.
Think not, O thou of little faith,
He"ll do much more, for me, for you?

Our times are in His blessed hands
Our food and raiment He'll supply;
He'll do abundantly and more,
If we but on His Word rely.

He'll give His angels charge o'er thee
To overshadow and protect.
He'll give His Spirit's grace and power
To fill, to comfort, and direct.

Mary D. Freeze

HE IS COMING

Oh, the joy of looking forward
To the day when Christ shall come,
To the glorious resurrection
Of the saints who've "overcome."

To the raptures of the Rapture,
Going up to be with Him
Through the ages of the ages
His sweet face will ne'er grow dim.

Yes, the world may scatter pleasures
That would thrill a human heart,
But the joy of seeing Jesus
Has no earthly counterpart.

It may take a little waiting
Till God's time is truly right,
But to know that He is coming
Fills the soul with pure delight.

Gladys M. Gearhart

God's Care

I KNOW HE IS REAL

I wish I could tell it — how wondrous is He
Who once died on Calv'ry, and now lives within me!
I cannot describe it just how I now **feel**,
But glory to Jesus! I know He is real!
The doubts are all settled; I'm His, yes, all His
The love of Jesus, how boundless it is!
It fills me and thrills me, and makes my heart glow,
I've joy in His service as I onward go.
His presence is with me, His Spirit abides,
He saves me and keeps me and always He guides,
He sanctifies wholly; O praise the dear Name
Of One who throughout ev'ry age is the same.
A full "yes" to Jesus I've said in my soul,
His precious Blood covers, His grace makes me whole,
I love Him, adore Him, in woe or in weal —
O praise Him forever! I know He is real!

"IT IS I, BE NOT AFRAID"

When the storm was fiercely raging
    On the lake of Galilee
And their helpless bark was tossing
    On the wild, tempestuous sea,
Walking on the raging waters
    In a robe of Light arrayed,
Jesus came, oh, hear Him calling
    "It is I, be not afraid!"

When the storms of life are raging,
    And the night is dark and drear,
When our strength is spent in toiling
    And our spirit sinks with fear,
Oft again we see Him coming,
    Swiftly hastening to our aid;
Often still we hear Him calling
    "It is I, be not afraid!"

When the night of death shall lower,
    And the Jordan's surges roll,
When the hour and power of darkness
    Overwhelm the sinking soul,
Then above the raging billows,
    And night's deepest, darkest shade,
We shall hear Him calling to us
    "It is I, be not afraid!"

A. B. Simpson

67

THE PILOT

As I sail o'er life's wide ocean,
  Speeding to eternity;
Christ, the One who never slumbers,
  Will my trusty Pilot be.

Hidden rocks I'm not alarmed at,
  Neither fear the bar of sand;
For I've given o'er the tiller,
  To the Pilot's steady hand.

Then through sunshine, rain or tempest,
  In the darkness or the day;
Though there be no track or pathway,
  Yet the Pilot knows the way.

Are you drifting, surely drifting,
  O'er life's wild and trackless sea?
Christ is calling o'er the billows,
  He your Pilot wants to be.

If you'll listen to His pleading,
  Though you see no port in sight;
He through simple faith will show you
  Bright and clear, the harbor light.

MY FRIEND

I have a friend so kind and true,
I want that you should know Him too.
'Tis Jesus Christ, God's only Son,
Blessed Saviour, most holy One.

He suffered, bled and died for me,
From sin and shame to set me free.
Living again, my burdens He bears —
Ready and willing to answer my prayers.

And even in death I'll have no fear,
For Jesus Christ is always near.
He'll gently take me by the hand
And lead me home to heaven's land.

68

My Friend is standing at your door.
He's been there many times before.
                    Marjorie Lorene Buster

HE CARES

Do your days seem long, your pleasures
    few;
  You have more griefs than your neigh-
    bors do;
The skies always cloudy, and never blue?
  Friend, go to God; He cares for you.

Your every task, they seem so long;
  You try to do right, but it turns out
    wrong;
There's never room in your heart for a
    song,
  Friend, go to Jesus; His arm is strong.

You smile as you start a brand-new day;
  But after awhile the smile goes away;
Everything goes, but the grief seems to
    stay.
  Friend, go to God, when you feel that
    way.

You start off the day so happy and free;
  But way in the distance more trouble
    you see,
So back to your state of perplexity flee;
  But Jesus has said, "Come unto me!"

There's only one way to lose all that care;
  To go through the day with a song in
    the air,
Slip down on your knees, in a moment of
    prayer,
  Wherever you meet Him, He's waiting
    there.
                    Owen C. Salway

GOD'S EYE IS ON THE SPARROW

Since God's eye is on the sparrow,
  Need I ever anxious be?
Should I needless trouble borrow
  When I know He cares for me?

Since God's eye is on the sparrow,
  And all things are in His hands,
I will trust Him for tomorrow,
  Gladly heeding His commands.

Since God's eye is on the sparrow
  And He watches over all,
I can walk the path, tho' narrow,
  Knowing He'll not let me fall.

Yes! God's eye is on the sparrow
  And He watches over me;
So I'll trust Him, ever trust Him,
  Since I know He cares for me.
                    Bertha Meyer

JESUS NEVER FAILS

Jesus never fails God's children
  As we journey on life's way,
Though sometimes the road seems
    rugged,
  And sometimes dark seems the day.

Satan is allowed to tempt us
  Till it seems that we may fall,
But the Master's ever near us
  And will hear the faintest call.

Jesus guards and guides us onward
  Calmly by the waters still,
Or along the thorny pathway,
  Leading higher up the hill.

Blessed be the name of Jesus;
  Let us sing His praises true;

For He dearly loves His children
  And will lead them safely through.
                    Walter E. Isenhour

HIS PRESENCE

I've walked along with Jesus
  These many days and years;
He's shared my joys, and sorrows,
  And wiped away my tears.

He's taught me many lessons
  By precept and by word;
By His restraining Spirit,
  And sometimes by the rod.

He's led me, gently led me
  Through pastures green and sweet,
And through afflictions trying
  And through the furnace heat.

His presence has not failed me;
  His promises have stood,
Like rocks, down underneath me
  When trials came, in floods.

He's heard me when I've asked Him
  For those who went astray;
And no good thing withheld from me
  As I walked in His own way.
                    Dale Schulz

HOW?

Leave the How with Jesus —
  'Tis enough to know
Faithful to His promise,
  Help He will bestow.
Leave the How with Jesus —
  He will all explain;
Only trust Him fully
  Till He comes again.

THE BEST FOR ME

I do not know what next may come
  Across my pilgrim way,
I do not know tomorrow's road,
  Nor see beyond today;
But this I know — My Saviour knows
  The path I cannot see,
And I can trust His wounded hand
  To guide and care for me.

I do not know what may befall
  Of sunshine or of rain,
I do not know what may be mine
  Of pleasure and of pain;
But this I know — my Saviour knows,
  And whatsoe'er it be,
Still I can trust His love to give
  What is best for me.

God's Touch

THE TOUCH OF THE MASTER'S HAND

'Twas battered and scarred, and the
    auctioneer
  Thought it scarcely worth his while
To waste much time on the old violin,
  But he held it up with a smile.
"What am I bidden, good folk?" he cried,
  "Who'll start the bidding for me?
"A dollar — a dollar — then two, only
    two —
  "Two dollars, and who'll make it three?
"Going for three" — but no —
  From the room far back, a gray-haired
    man
Came forward and picked up the bow,
  Then, wiping the dust from the old
    violin,
And tightening the loosened strings,
  He played a melody pure and sweet
As a caroling angel sings.

The music ceased, and the auctioneer,
  With a voice that was quiet and low,
Said, "*Now* what am I bid for the old
    violin?"
  And he held it up with the bow.
"A thousand dollars — and who'll make
    it two?

"Two thousand — and who'll make it
    three?
"Three thousand once — three thousand
    twice —
  "And going — and gone," cried he.
The people cheered, but some of them
    cried,
  "We do not understand.
"What changed its worth?"—Quick came
    the reply,
  "The touch of the Master's hand."

And many a man with life out of tune,
  And battered and scarred with sin,
Is auctioned cheap, to a thoughtless
    crowd,
  Much like the old violin.
A "mess of pottage" — a glass of wine,
  A game — and he travels on:
He is going once — and going twice —
  He's going — and almost gone!
But the Master comes, and the foolish
    crowd
  Never can quite understand
The worth of a soul, and the change that's
    wrought
  By *the touch of the Master's hand.*

WIT'S-END CORNER

Are you standing at Wit's-End Corner,
  Christian with troubled brow?
Are you thinking of what is before you,
  And all you are bearing now?
Does all the world seem against you,
  And you in the battle alone?
Remember — at Wit's-End Corner
  Is just where God's power is shown.

Are you standing at Wit's-End Corner
  Blinded with wearying pain,
Feeling you cannot endure it,
  You cannot bear the strain?
Bruised through the constant suffering,
  Dizzy and dazed and dumb?
Remember — at Wit's-End Corner
  Is where Jesus loves to come.

Are you standing at Wit's-End Corner
  Your work before you spread,
All lying begun, unfinished,
  And pressing on heart and head,
Longing for strength to do it,
  Stretching out trembling hands?
Remember — at Wit's-End Corner
  The Burden-bearer stands.

Are you standing at Wit's-End Corner?
  Then you're just in the very spot
To learn the wondrous resources
  Of Him who faileth not.
No doubt, to a brighter pathway
  Your footsteps will soon be moved.
But only at Wit's-End Corner
  Is the "God who is able" proved.

TELL JESUS

When thou wakest in the morning,
  Ere thou tread the untried way
Of the lot that lies before thee,
  Through the coming busy day,
Whether sunbeams promise brightness,
  Whether dim forebodings fall,
Be thy dawning glad or gloomy,
  Go to Jesus — tell Him all!

In the calm of sweet communion
  Let thy daily work be done;
In the peace of soul outpouring,
  Care be banished, patience won;
And if earth, with its enchantments,
  Seek the spirit to enthrall,
Ere thou listen, ere thou answer,
  Turn to Jesus — tell Him all!

Then, as hour by hour glides by thee,
  Thou wilt blessed guidance know;
Thine own burdens being lightened,
  Thou canst bear another's woe;
Thou canst help the weak ones onward
  Thou canst raise up those that fall;
But remember, while thou servest,
  Still tell Jesus — tell Him all!

And if weariness creep o'er thee
  As the day wears to its close,
Or if sudden fierce temptation
  Brings thee face to face with foes,
In thy weakness, in thy peril,
  Raise to heaven a trustful call;
Strength and calm for every crisis
  Come — in telling Jesus all!

IT'S WONDERFUL

It's wonderful, so wonderful,
  To be a child of God,
And walk the Christian path of life
  O'er which the saints have trod;
To have God's grace down in our soul
  That keeps us kind and sweet,
And helps us bless our loved ones dear
  And those we chance to meet.

It's wonderful to love mankind —
  No hatred in our heart —
With no desire to put men down
  By word and fiery dart;
But reaching forth a hand to lift
  We help the fallen rise,
And seek the Lord for saving grace
  Who clears his mortal skies.

It's wonderful to sing and pray
  While others fret and frown,
And feel God's peace within our heart
  And heaven smiling down;
To know we have the victory
  O'er sins that grip the world;
That we are soldiers for our Lord
  Beneath His flag unfurled.

Walter E. Isenhour

ABIDING

I have learned the wondrous secret
  Of abiding in the Lord;
I have found the strength and sweetness
  Of confiding in His Word.
I have tasted life's pure fountain,
  I am trusting in His blood;
I have lost myself in Jesus,
  I am sinking into God.

I am crucified with Jesus,
  And He lives and dwells with me;
I have ceased from all my struggling.
  'Tis no longer I but He.
All my will is yielded to Him,
  And His Spirit reigns within;
And His precious blood each moment,
  Keeps me cleansed and free from sin.

For my words, I take His wisdom
  For my works, His Spirit's power,
For my ways, His ceaseless Presence
  Guides and guards me every hour.
Of my heart, He is the Portion,
  Of my joy, the boundless Spring;
Saviour, Sanctifier, Healer,
  Glorious Lord, and coming King!

A. B. Simpson

God's Way

GOD KNOWS THE ANSWER

I question not God's means or ways,
Or how He uses time or days,
To answer every call or prayer,
I know He will, somehow, somewhere.

I question not the time or place
When I shall feel His love and grace;

I only know that I believe,
And richest blessings shall receive.

I cannot doubt that He'll attend
My every call, and that He'll send
A ministering angel fair,
In answer to my faithful prayer.

F. B. Whitney

SOMETIMES

Sometimes the lions' mouths are shut;
Sometimes God bids us fight or fly;
Sometimes He feeds us by the brook;
Sometimes the flowing stream runs dry.

Sometimes the burning flames are
   quenched
Sometimes with sevenfold heat they
   glow;
Sometimes His hand divides the waves;
Sometimes His billows overflow.

Sometimes He turns the sword aside;
Sometimes He lets the sharp blade
   smite;
Sometimes our foes are at our heels,
Sometimes He hides us from their sight.

We may not choose, nor would we dare,
The path in which our feet shall tread;
Enough that He that path hath made,
And He Himself shall walk ahead.

The danger that His love allows
Is safer than our fears may know;
The peril that His care permits
Is our defence where'er we go.
Annie Johnson Flint

DAY BY DAY

Day by day, oh Master, make me
  With that blessed life of Thine,
Day by day, oh Lord, enfold me
  With Thy mighty grace divine.
Day by day, oh Saviour, take me
  For Thy servant, willing, free,
Day by day, oh Master, make me
  All that Thou wouldst have me be.
Day by day, oh Saviour, keep me
  Just abiding in Thy love,

Simply trusting and obeying,
  Looking unto Thee above.
Day by day, oh Saviour, give me
  All the strength I need so much,
And with Thee and Thy blest Spirit,
  Ever keep me, Lord, in touch.
Day by day, to fight the battle,
  Day by day, Thy will to do,
Day by day, the cross to carry,
  Seeking only to be true.
Help me, Lord, to leave the future
  Safe within Thy hands for aye,
Trusting Thee, Lord, to renew me,
  Living simply day by day.
A. G. Fisher

HE MAKETH NO MISTAKE

My Father's way may twist and turn,
  My heart may throb and ache,
But in my soul I'm glad I know,
  He maketh no mistake.

My cherished plans may go astray,
  My hopes may fade away,
But still I'll trust my Lord to lead
  For He doth know the way.

Though night be dark and it may seem
  That day will never break;
I'll pin my faith, my all in Him,
  He maketh no mistake.

There's so much now I cannot see,
  My eyesight's far too dim;
But come what may, I'll simply trust
  And leave it all to Him.

For by and by the mist will lift
  And plain it all He'll make,
Through all the way, though dark to me,
  He made not one mistake.
A. M. Overton

73

MOURNING

I have sunk to the cold weary depths of
   despair!
   Death at last has struck one of my own.
And the grief that I've felt has been
   heavy to bear;
   I could never have borne it alone.

But my God in His grace — oh, what
   marvelous grace!
   Holds me close to His comforting
   breast;
And I know that my loved one now
   stands in that place
   In His wonderful haven of rest.

And so now in some strange and mys-
   terious way
   God has taken the grief I have known
And reshaped it, as though it were soft
   supple clay,
   Into peace from His merciful throne.
            Josephine Van Fossan

GOD KNOWS WHAT HE'S ABOUT

When God wants to drill a man,
And thrill a man, and skill a man;
When God wants to mold a man
To play the noblest part;
When He yearns with all His heart
To create so great and bold a man
That all the world shall be amazed,
Watch His methods, watch His ways
How He ruthlessly perfects
Whom He royally elects!
How He hammers him or hurts him
And with mighty blows converts him
Into trial shapes of clay which
Only God can understand.

THY WILL BE DONE
Matthew 6:10

This is the safest prayer to pray:
   "Thy will be done";
Along the world's unlighted way
   Where unseen dangers run.
So, though for all the saints we pray,
   Or but for one,
Upon this rock our hearts may stay,
   His will shall yet be done.

This is the surest way to pray:
   "Thy will be done";
Along the world's uncertain way
   Where crowded terrors run.
For though our dearest plans may fail,
   Our hopes die one by one,
Though heaven and earth shall pass away
   His will shall yet be done.
            Annie Johnson Flint

STEP BY STEP

He does not lead me year by year
Nor even day by day,
But step by step my path unfolds;
My Lord directs my way.

Tomorrow's plans I do not know,
I only know this minute;
But He will say, "This is the way,
By faith now walk ye in it."

And I am glad it is so,
Today's enough to bear;
And when tomorrow comes, His grace
Shall far exceed its care.

What need to worry then, or fret?
The God who gave His Son
Holds all my moments in His hand
And gives them, one by one.
            Barbara C. Ryberg

HIS PLAN

Before He formed a star,
  Our God arranged our lot;
Our little lives were planned afar,
  When we as yet were not.

Time hath no aimless strands,
  God's warp and woof combines;
Life's loom is in His holy hands,
  His shuttles know their lines.

He purposed all He sends,
  He knows what us awaits;
He marketh now the distant ends
  Of paths to hidden gates.

All acts His eyes foresee
  And never choice constrain;
So willeth He that we are free
  His grace to lose or gain.

His love hath filled the past,
  An ocean without shore;
Our purchased souls Him first and last
  Love, trust, obey, adore.

Author Unknown

God's Will

GOD'S WILL IS BEST

God's will is better than our will,
  It's always right and good.
I would not have my way at all,
  Not even if I could.
God holds the future in His hands
  And scans the unspent years;
He knows the trying hours ahead,
  The pain and bitter tears.

Oh! just to leave it all with Him
  And lean upon His breast.
To know, whatever comes or goes,
  That His dear will is best.
Oh! just to let Him have His way,
  With heart and life and soul,
Brings peace so sweet and joy divine,
  And leads us safely Home.

We cannot understand, sometimes,
  Why things do happen so,
Nor why the way is often rough
  That we are called to go.

But in the meadow's sunlight
  Or through the mountain's cleft,
Hold Him gently by the hand
  And know His will is best.

Thelma Curtis

AFTER THE DARK

After the dark the dawn,
After the night the day,
After the storm of grief
A faith to put away

Into the heart where love,
Still a vibrant thing,
Draws the bow of hope
Across a viol's string

And waken once again
Peace to calm the strife,
And show that God is still
Holding the reins of life.

Enola Chamberlain

GOD'S KEY

Is there some problem in your life to
   solve,
   Some passage seeming full of mystery?
God knows, who brings the hidden thing
   to light.
   He keeps the key.

Is there some door closed by the Father's
   Hand
   Which widely opened you had hoped
   to see?
Trust God and wait — for when He shuts
   the door
   He keeps the key.

Is there some earnest prayer unanswered
   yet,
   Or answered not as you had thought
   'twould be?
God will make clear His purpose by and
   by.
   He keeps the key.

Have patience with your God, your
   patient God
   All wise, all knowing, no long tarrier
   He.
And of the door of all thy future life.
   He keeps the key.

Unfailing comfort, sweet and blessed rest,
   To know of every door He keeps the
   key.
That He at last when just He sees 'tis
   best
   Will give it thee.

THY WILL BE DONE
(Luke 22:42)

Why did He choose a garden fair,
   When bowed in agony?
Would not a hillside, barren, cold,
   Be more in harmony?

Ah no! The gracious Lord of love
   Would have His children know
That in their darkest hours of pain,
   The fragrant flowers grow —

That there, amid the sharpest thorns,
   The rarest roses bloom,
And there the richness of His grace
   Dispels the deepest gloom.

His anguished heart was torn with pain;
   None else could suffer so,
Yet in our deepest agony
   This much our hearts can know —

That in our anguish and our pain
   The victory can be won
If we will say as He once said:
   "Thy will, Thy will be done."

What though tomorrow has its cross?
   Naught can His love e'er dim;
From out the depths of deepest woe
   We gladly walk with Him.

Then to the garden let us go —
   The garden of God's will,
Content to know, where'er He leads
   That we can trust Him still.

Albert Simpson Reitz

THE BEST FOR US

God knew what lay before us
   In the days that have gone by;
He knew each step that we would take;
   He saw with watchful eye.
He knew the road was oft-times steep
   And the traveling rough and slow,
But He planned the very best for us,
   Ah, many years ago!

He knew our hearts were often faint
   And our eyes with tears were dim;
There wasn't anything at all
   That was not known to Him.
He knew the longing of our hearts,
   Our doubts and hopes and fears,
But, oh, He planned the best for us,
   We saw it through our tears!

And so, our hearts are full of thanks,
   They're full of love and praise,
Because He's been our Guard and Guide
   Through all our yesterdays.
And in the days that lie ahead,
   We're sure He'll be our stay,
For He has planned the best for us
   And will lead us all the way!
               Olive H. Burnett

HIS PLAN FOR ME

When I stand at the judgment seat of
   Christ
   And He shows me His plan for me,
The plan of my life as it might have been
   Had He had His way, and I see.
How I blocked Him here, and I checked
   Him there,
   And I would not yield my will,
Will there be grief in my Saviour's eyes,
   Grief, though He loves me still?
He would have made me rich, and I stand
   there poor,
   Stripped of all but His grace,
While memory runs like a hunted thing
   Down the paths I cannot retrace.
Then my desolate heart will well-nigh
   break
   With the tears that I cannot shed;
I shall cover my face with my empty
   hands,
   I shall bow my uncrowned head.
Lord, of the years that are left me,
   I give them to Thy hand:
Take me and break me, mould me to
   The pattern Thou hast planned.
             Martha Snell Nicholso

God With Us

A GIFT OF GOD

That I should have a joyous life
   In this old world below,
Amid the turmoil and the strife,
   Is a gift of God, I know.

He shows His love each day to me
   Through countless blessings here —

A happy home and family,
   And friends so kind and dear;

A peace that deep within me lives,
   As through my daily tasks I go.
The joy that only Jesus gives
   Makes life worth living here below!

I SEE GOD

I see God in the bluebird's wing;
I hear His voice when robins sing;
I see His smile in the rainbow's glow;
I hear His steps on the crusted snow.

I see God's tears in the morning dew;
I see His face when day is new;
I see His love in pink rose bush,
His calmness in the evening hush.

I feel His power in lightning flash,
His anger in the thunder's crash,
His thoughtfulness in the gentle rain,
His loving care in the ripening grain.

With eyes that see He's everywhere,
With ears that hear He's always near—
Leading us out of our wilderness,
Guiding with strength and tenderness.

OUR CHRIST

I know not how that Bethlehem's Babe
  Could in the Godhead be;
I only know the Manger Child
  Has brought God's life to me.

I know not how that Calvary's cross
  A world from sin could free;
I on'ly know its matchless love
  Has brought God's love to me.

I know not how that Joseph's tomb
  Could solve death's mystery,
I only know a living Christ,
  Our immortality!

Harry Webb Farrington

THE SPARROW'S SONG

I'm only a little sparrow,
  A bird of low degree;
My life is of little value,
  But the dear Lord cares for me.
He gives me a coat of feathers —
  It is very plain I know,
Without a speck of crimson,
  For it was not made for show.
But it keeps me warm in winter,
  And it shields me from the rain;
Were it bordered with gold and purple,
  Perhaps it would make me vain.

BECAUSE HE WAS TEMPTED

He knows when shadows come my way
  And penetrate my path.
He knows when I'm the recipient
  Of someone's stinging wrath.

He knows when others do rejoice
  When hopes are swept away.
He knows as does no other
  When words do whip and flay.

He knows the heartache and the woe
  Of false accusation too.
There's not a thing that can happen
  But that He has been through.

He knows because He was tempted
  In all points like as we.
We have such a loving High Priest
  A refuge to whom we flee.

Holy Spirit

"TARRY YE"

"Tarry," said the Master, "till the power
  God gives you is bestowed." They
  waited there
Within the upper room in faith and
  patience.
  And Pentecost was answered to their
  prayer.

Oh, give us grace to tarry in this hour,
  To wait Thy summons, Lord, to hear
  Thy Word.
Check our impetuous haste, remembering
  always,
  What is Thy will can never be deferred.

In quietness and confidence, strength-
  giving,
  We would realize Thy presence and
  deny
Our tears in this Thy promise, "I will
  teach thee
  The way to go and guide thee with
  mine eye."

HOLY SPIRIT, LEAD ME

Holy Spirit, lead me,
  In God's will today,
With His manna feed me,
  Lest I go astray.

Holy Spirit, guide me,
  On His paths aright;
From all evil hide me,
  Perfect in His sight.

Holy Spirit, guard me,
  Both from foe and friend,
Keep me from temptation
  To the very end.

Holy Spirit, teach me,
  All I need to know,
That my life may please Him
  Everywhere I go.

Home

FAMILY

The family is a little book,
  The children are the leaves,
The parents are the cover that
  Safe protection gives.

At first, the pages of the book
  Are blank, and smooth, and fair;

But time soon writeth memories,
  And painteth pictures there.

Love is the golden clasp
  That bindeth up the trust;
O break it not, lest all the leaves
  Shall scatter like the dust.

THE FAMILY ALTAR

The family altar in our home
  Holds such a beauty rare;
Among the treasures of this life
  There's none that can compare.

'Tis just about the evening hour
  When day has spent itself
That Dad takes down the Bible
  From its place upon the shelf.

We read the Word together and
  We bow at Jesus' feet;
How precious is that fellowship!
  It makes our day complete!

And all the burdens we possess
  Are swallowed up in prayer;
The sweetness of this time with God
  Reveals His love and care.

A family altar in the home!
  How blessed and how true
That if we put God first — He'll bless!
  We hope you have one too!

Georgia B. Adams

A HOME PRAYER

Lord of all pots and pans and things,
  Since I've no time to be
A saint by doing lovely deeds
  Or watching late with Thee:
Or dreaming in the dawnlight
  Or storming heaven's gates,
Make me a saint by getting meals
  And washing up the plates!

Although I must have Martha's hands
  I have a Mary mind,
And when I black the boots and shoes,
  Thy sandals, Lord, I find!

I think of how they trod the earth,
  What time I scrub the floor;
Accept this meditation, Lord!
  I haven't time for more.

Warm all the kitchen with Thy love,
  And light it with Thy peace!
Forgive me all my worrying
  And make all grumbling cease!
Thou who didst love to give men food
  In a room or by the sea,
Accept this service that I do —
  I do it unto Thee!

HOME

Our earthly homes are simple things
  Of plaster and of board,
Sometimes as humble as the nest
  Built by a wildwood bird.

And yet through all our lives our hearts
  Cling to this childhood home
Of hallowed, precious memories,
  No matter where we roam.

And so I often think about
  How dear, how very dear,
Our heavenly home will come to be
  With every passing year.

That home where we shall meet and dwell
  With loved ones gone before,
And sometimes, looking up, shall see
  Our Lord come through the door.

Sweet home, where all our fulfilled joys
  Become rich memories,
And ever deeper pleasures crowd
  The long eternities!

Martha Snell Nicholson

TRUE RICHES

What tho' thy home
  Be humble and small,
Dwarfed by thy neighbor's,
  Costly and fine?
All of the world
  And its fullness is Mine,
And you are My child,
  Far richer than all!

Why do you look
  With yearning of heart
On his luxuries, leisure,
  His comfort and ease?
Thy rest of salvation
  Is better than these!
He knows not the joy
  Only grace can impart!

Pity, instead,
  The dearth of his soul,
Seeking vain pleasure,
  Striving for gain,
Knowing no comfort
  Nor solace for pain,
Caught in the web
  Of the devil's control.

He is rich in the goods,
  That the world can bestow,
But poor in the things
  Eternal and true!
Show him, My child,
  By the wealth I give you,
There are riches far greater
  Than his he can know!

Bessie June Martin

HOME

I turned an ancient poet's book,
  And found upon the page,
"Stone walls do not a prison make,
  Or iron bars a cage."

Yes, that is true, and something more
  You will find where'er you roam . . .
That marble floors and gilded walls
  Can never make a home.
But everywhere that love abides,
  And friendship is a guest,
Is surely home, and home, sweet home,
  For there the soul can rest.

Henry van Dyke

THE SWEETEST HOME

The sweetest home is a little home,
  With a dear little mother in it;
And if in your heart there's a little song
  For the mother you love, begin it;
For this is her hour and this her day,
  Though she's living afar or near you;
In a mansion fair or a shack out there,
  The mother you love will hear you!

The sweetest home is a quiet home,
  With a peace that a mother wills it;
And you're still her child, though you're
    far away,
  For she holds to your heart and fills it
With the memories of a time gone by
  When you whispered the prayers she
    taught you;
And she can't forget, though her eyes be
    wet,
  How great was the price that bought
    you.

The sweetest home is a God-blest home
  That rests near a humble by-way,
And always the fairest one within
  Is a mother who shuns the highway
Where evil struts in a robe of red,
  Where devilish imps will call you.
Go back to her knee, to her warm arms
    flee,
  And never shall ill befall you!

Hope

NEW EVERY MORNING

Every day is a fresh beginning,
  Every morn is the world made new;
You who are weary of sorrow and sinning,
  Here is a beautiful hope for you —
  A hope for me and a hope for you.

All the past things are past and over,
  The tasks are done and the tears are
    shed;
Yesterday's errors let yesterday cover;
  Yesterday's wounds, which smarted
    and bled,
  Are healed with the healing which
    night has shed.

Yesterday is a part of forever,
  Bound up in a sheaf which God holds
    tight;
With glad days and sad days and bad
    days which never
  Shall visit us more with their bloom
    and their blight,
  Their fullness of sunshine or sorrowful
    night.

Let them go, since we cannot relieve
    them;
  Cannot undo, and cannot atone;
God in His mercy, receive, forgive them!
  Only the new days are our own.
  Today is ours, and today alone.

Here are the skies all burnished brightly,
  Here is the spent earth all reborn;
Here are the tired limbs springing lightly
To face the sun, and to share with the
    morn
In the prism of dew and the cool of
    dawn.

A SONG OF LOW DEGREE

He that is down need fear no fall;
  He that is low, no pride;
He that is humble ever shall
  Have God to be his guide.

I am content with what I have,
  Little be it or much;
And, Lord, contentment still I crave,
  Because thou savest such.

Fullness to such a burden is
  That go on pilgrimage;
Here little, and hereafter bliss,
  Is best from age to age.
                    John Bunyan

WAIT ON !

To talk with God,
No breath is lost —
  Talk on!

To walk with God,
No strength is lost —
  Walk on!

To wait on God,
No time is lost —
  Wait on!

Joy

SECRET OF SONG

Why do I sing in the morning,
When the skies are gloomy and gray;
Faithfully trusting my Master,
Though showers dampen my way?

Why am I humming at noontime,
Letting no discord come in,
Keeping my mind calm and quiet,
Banishing Satan and sin?

Why do I smile in the evening,
Making my world new and bright;
And ever pray in darkness,
Knowing dawn comes after night?

Here's why I'm singing and smiling,
While angels carol above:
Christ found my heart full of sorrow,
Cleansed it and filled it with love.

Christine White

GIVE MY HEART A SONG

Lord of comfort, hope, and love,
Give my heart a song;
A song of radiance and cheer
As I march along.
Help me to sing a joyful song
For those bowed down with care;
A song of hope and freedom
For those in dark despair.
Help me to sing a valiant song
For those who mope and sigh;
A song to stir the hearts of men
'Ere I shall pass them by!

Anna M. Gilleland

LIFE'S JOY

God gives us joy that we might give;
    He gives us love that we may share;
Sometimes He gives us loads to lift
    That we may learn to bear.
For life is gladder when we give,
    And love is sweeter when we share,
And heavy loads rest lightly, too,
    When we have learned to bear.

JUST TO BE GLAD

Just to be glad I am living,
    Just to be glad is sweet;
Just to be glad for my loved ones,
    And for friends whom we meet.

Just to be glad for the sunshine,
    And for the thunderstorms too;
Glad for the calm of twilight
    And for the morning's fresh dew.

Glad in life's bitter-sweet sorrows.
    Glad for the comfort God sends.
Glad for the hope of reunion
    Ours, when earth's happiness ends.

Just to be glad! What a blessing!
    Joy divine floods our way,
Driving away every sorrow,
    Brightening the loveliest day.

Father, the giver of gladness,
    Hearts of thanksgiving we raise,
Asking for lives filled with sweetness,
    Gratitude, gladness and praise.

Merlin G. Miller

83

HAPPINESS

It's not so much the things without,
  The things you may possess,
As money, riches, houses, land,
  That make for happiness;
Although the world may think so
  And seeks to thus attain,
Or strives for other outward things —
  At last we find them in vain.

A mind that's filled with noble thoughts,
  A heart that's fixed on God;
A will to do the honest things
  And walk where Jesus trod;
A purpose great, an aim that's high,
  A soul that's clear of sin —
This brings a happiness so sweet,
  And springs up from within!

Walter Isenhour

Kindness

LIFE IS SO SHORT

Let's smile and be kind — life is so short
  And most of the way so rough,
The times are trying, the road upgrade,
  And always trouble enough.
Yesterday's hurts we'll try to forego —
  And tomorrow's cares can wait,
Today with diligence let us keep
  Our hearts from the strain of hate.

Life is too short for spite and revenge,
  And paying back wrong for wrong;
Try patience and love and forgiveness,
  Meet slights with a smile and a song.
The sad world with all its repining,
  Its bitterness, care and tears,
Needs the wealth of your loving kindness
  To sweeten the sin-soiled years.

Yes, life is too short to be hateful,
  Or scorning any you meet,
Then strive to be pleasant and gentle,
  Always to smile and be sweet;
For the sunshine of love is needed
  To warm the world with its light,
And to shed abroad its effulgence
  To bless humanity's night.

Margaret S. Hall

BE CAREFUL WHAT YOU SAY

In speaking of a person's faults,
  Pray don't forget your own;
Remember those with homes of glass
  Should seldom throw a stone.
If we have nothing else to do
  But talk of those who sin,
'Tis better we commence at home,
  And from that point begin.
We have no right to judge a man
  Until he's fairly tried;
Should we not like his company,
  We know the world is wide.
Some may have faults—and who has not?
  The old as well as young;
Perhaps we may, for aught we know
  Have fifty to their one.
Then let us all, when we begin
  To slander friend or foe,
Think of the harm one word may do
  To those we little know.
Remember curses sometimes like
  Our chickens "roost at home";
Don't speak of others' faults until
  We have none of our own.

Joseph Kronthal

THE BEST MEMORY COURSE

Forget each kindness that you do as soon
    as you have done it;
Forget the praise that falls to you the
    moment you have won it;
Forget the slander that you hear before
    you can repeat it;
Forget each slight, each spit, each sneer,
    whenever you may meet it.
Remember every kindness done to you
    whate'er its measure:
Remember praise by others won and pass
    it on with pleasure:
Remember every promise made and keep
    it to the letter:
Remember those who lend you aid and
    be a grateful debtor.
Remember all the happiness that comes
    your way in living:
Remember each worry and distress, be
    hopeful and forgiving:
Remember good, remember truth, remem-
    ber heaven's above you,
And you will find, through age and youth,
    That many hearts will love you.

THE DIFFERENCE

Drop an unkind word or careless —
    Just a flash and it is gone,
But a half a hundred ripples
    Go a-circling on and on;
They keep spreading, spreading,
    spreading
    From the center as they go,
And there is no way to stop them,
    Once you've started them to flow.

Drop an unkind word or careless —
    In a minute you forget,
But it started waves to flowing
    And its ripples circle yet:

And perhaps in some sad pilgrim
    A great wave of tears you've stirred,
And disturbed a life that's happy
    When you dropped that unkind word.

Drop a word of cheer and kindness —
    Just a flash and it is gone,
But a half a hundred ripples
    Go a-circling on and on,
Bearing hope and joy and comfort
    On each splashing, dashing wave,
Till you can't conceive the volume
    Of the kind word that you gave.

Drop a word of cheer and kindness —
    In a minute you forget,
But the gladness that it started
    Swells and circles even yet;
And you've rolled a wave of comfort,
    Whose sweet music can be heard
Over miles and miles of water,
    Just by dropping a kind word.
             The Gideon

KINDNESS DURING LIFE

I would rather have one little rose
    From the garden of a friend,
Than to have the choicest flowers
    When my stay on earth must end.
I would rather have a pleasant word
    In kindness said to me,
Than flattery when my heart is still
    And life has ceased to be.
I would rather have a loving smile
    From friends I know are true,
Than tears shed 'round my casket
    When this world I've bid adieu.
Bring me all your flowers today
    Whether pink, or white, or red,
I'd rather have one blossom now
    Than a truck load when I'm dead.

ONLY A SMILE

Only a smile that was given me
  On the crowded street one day,
But pierced the gloom of my saddened
    heart
  Like a sudden sunbeam's ray.
The shadow of doubt hung o'er me,
  And the burden of pain I bore,
And the voice of hope I could not hear,
  Though I listened o'er and o'er.

But there came a rift in the crowd about
  And a face I knew passed by,
And the smile I caught was brighter to
    me
  Than the blue of a summer sky;
For it gave me back the sunshine,
  And it scattered each somber thought,
And my heart rejoiced in the kindly
    warmth
  Which that kindly smile had wrought.

Only a smile from a kindly face
  On the busy street that day!
Forgotten as soon as given perhaps,
  As the donor went her way,
But straight to my heart it went speeding,
  To gild the clouds that were there:
And I found that of sunshine and life's
    blue skies,
  I also might take my share.

LITTLE THINGS

It was only a kindly smile he gave
  As he passed along the way
But it lifted a load from a weary heart
  And brightened a dreary day.

It was only a cheery word he spoke
  But it made his brother strong
And gave him courage anew to tread
  The road he must walk along.

It was only a helping hand he gave
  To a struggler on life's road
Who was struggling on through the weary
    way
  So tired beneath life's load.

Such little things in the world's cold eye,
  But the Master he served could see
The love in his heart, and He whispered
    low,
  "Ye have done it unto Me."

SLOW ME DOWN

Slow me down, Lord. I am going too fast;
I can't see my brother when he's walking
  past.
I miss a lot of good things day by day;
I don't know a blessing when it comes
  my way.

Slow me down, Lord. I want to see
More of the things that are good for me.
A little less of me and a little more of
  You,
I want the heavenly atmosphere to trickle
  through.

Let me help a brother when the going is
  rough;
When folks work together life isn't so
  tough.
Slow me down, Lord, so I can talk
With some of Your angels as they walk.

KINDNESS

Be swift, dear heart, in saying
  The kindly word;
When ears are sealed thy passionate
    pleading
  Will not be heard.

Be swift, dear heart, in doing
  The gracious deed;
Lest soon, they whom thou holdest
    dearest
  Be past thy need.

86

DO SOMETHING

Do something for somebody somewhere
　　While jogging along life's road;
Help someone to carry his burden,
　　And lighter will grow your load!

Do something for somebody gladly,
　　'Twill sweeten your every care;
In sharing the sorrows of others,
　　Your own are less hard to bear.

Do something for somebody, striving
　　To help where the way seems long.
And the sorrowful hearts that languish
　　Cheer up with a little song.

Do something for somebody always,
　　Whatever may be your creed,
There's nothing on earth can help you
　　So much as a kindly deed!

Men

IF YOU'RE THE MAN
YOU OUGHT TO BE

If you're the man you ought to be
　　You "carry fair" with ev'ry man,
You take no undermining scheme
　　And lay no cunning, selfish plan
By which to gain some cash or wealth,
　　Or reach a place that's figured high;
You'd rather have a conscience clear
　　Than all that wrong could give or buy.

If you're the man you ought to be
　　You're clean in spirit, heart and mind;
You're noble in your heart and great,
　　And great because you're meek and
　　　kind.
You're not a lying hypocrite,
　　A glitter in your outer shine;
A "cover up," a "make believe,"
　　A false director by your sign.

If you're the man you ought to be
　　You do not curse, nor drink, nor lie;
You have a higher aim and plan
　　Than to exist and just get by.
You want God's blessings on your life,
　　And then you want to bless mankind;
You live to fill your place on earth
　　Where Providence to you assigned.

If you're the man you ought to be
　　You treat your family as you should;
You're kind at home and love your folks,
　　And love and bless your neighborhood.
You're honest as you deal with men,
　　And honest with the God you serve;
You love His church and righteous cause
　　And give with no unjust reserve.

　　　　　　　Walter E. Isenhour

MEASURE OF SUCCESS

When sunset falls upon your day
And fades from out the west,
When business cares are put away
And you lie down to rest,
The measure of the day's success
Or failure may be told
In terms of human happiness
And not in terms of gold.

Is there beside some hearth tonight
More joy because you wrought?
Does someone face the bitter fight
With courage you have taught?
Is something added to the store
Of human happiness?
If so, the day that now is o'er
Has been a real success.

87

SOME THINGS YOU CANNOT WILL TO MEN

You cannot will to men your health,
  Your knowledge and your learning
Which some might value more than
    wealth
  For which they may be yearning;
For there are treasures we possess
  That we can't will to others,
Although 'twould be so great to bless
  With these our friends and brothers.

You cannot will to men your face,
  Your character that's shining;
You cannot will to them your grace
  That's taken much refining;
Nor can you give to them your peace
  You've found in God's salvation,
Along with blessings that increase
  That help your land and nation.

There's that which men must earn them-
    selves
  Through years of work and study,
Which can't be handed down from
    shelves,
  Nor granted by a buddy;
Therefore the earning must be yours,
  Or the gift must be divine;
Then seek the place where heaven pours
  Her wealth on humankind.
          Walter E. Isenhour

MEASURING A MAN

The man's no bigger than the way he
  treats his fellow man.
This standard has his measure been since
  time itself began!
He's measured not by race or creed, high
  sounding though they be;
Nor by the gold that's put aside, nor by
  his sanctity!

He's measured not by social rank when
  character's the test;
Nor by his earthly pomp or show, dis-
  playing wealth possessed.
He's measured by his justice, right, his
  fairness at his play;
His squareness in all dealings made, his
  honest upright way.
These are his measures, ever near, to
  serve him when they can;
For man's no bigger than the way he
  treats his fellow man.

MEASURE OF A MAN

Not, how did he die?
But, how did he live?
Not, what did he gain?
But, what did he give?

These are the merits
To measure the worth
Of a man as a man
Regardless of birth.

Not, what was his station?
But, had he a heart?
And how did he play
His God-given part?

Was he ever ready
With a word of good cheer
To bring a smile,
To banish a tear?

Not, what was his church?
Nor, what was his creed?
But had he befriended
Those really in need?

Not, what did the sketch
In the newspaper say?
But, how many were sorry
When he passed away?

GIVE US SOBER MEN

Give us sober men for leaders —
Men who never take a drink;
Men who love our God and country,
And whose minds are clear to think;
Men who strive to do their duty
In the places that they fill;
Men who can't be bought with money,
Nor with evils that would thrill.

Give us sober men in business
Whom, as patrons, we can trust;
Men whose characters are spotless
And whose plans are fair and just;
Men who live the truth and tell it —
Free from pretense and disguise;
Men whose aim and work and purpose
Is to help their fellows rise.

Give us sober men in business —
Men who love our country's laws;
Men who stand for righteous freedom
And for ev'ry noble cause;
Men with hearts both kind and tender
Toward their fellows that are down;
Men who wouldn't sell their nation
For a throne and robe and crown.

Give us sober men as fathers,
Sober teachers for our schools;
Men with sound, exalted standards,
Far removed from those of fools;
Men who love the Holy Bible
And obey it, day by day;
Give us men to lead us upward —
Men who watch and fast and pray.

Walter E. Isenhour

FOR EVERY MAN

There is a niche provided
For every man;
Each makes his contribution
In God's great plan;
Let no one feel superfluous
In that vast scheme,
However small and hidden
His life may seem.
Some must go forth to battle;
Some mind the camp;
Some cross the mighty billows;
Some tend the lamp,
And keep their lonely vigil
Till break of day,
To guide some storm-tossed vessel
Upon its way.
Some serve their generation;
Some, those unborn;
Some lose their lives in secret
Like buried corn;
Some sow their fields with weeping;
Some reap the grain
And fill their barns with plenty
From others' pain.
Dear Master, Thine appointments
To me are sweet,
If I'm but for Thy service
A vessel meet;
In labors more abundant,
Or out of sight,
Thine openings and shuttings
Are always right.

Max I. Reich

Mother

A KITCHEN PRAYER

God bless my little kitchen,
I love its every nook
And God bless me as I do my work,
Wash pots and pans and cook.

And may the meals that I prepare
Be successful from above
With Thy blessing and Thy grace
But most of all Thy love.

As we partake of earthly good
The table before us spread
We'll not forget to thank Thee, Lord,
Who gives us daily bread.

So bless my little kitchen, Lord,
And those who enter in
May they find naught but joy and peace
And happiness therein.

M. Petersen

ARE ALL THE CHILDREN IN?

I think oft times as night draws nigh
Of the old farmhouse on the hill,
Of a yard all wide and blossom-starred
Where the children played at will.
And when the night at last came down
Hushing the merry din,
Mother would look around and ask,
"Are all the children in?"

Tis many and many a year since then,
And the house on the hill
No longer echoes to children's feet
And the yard is still, so still.

But I see it all, the shadows creep,
And though many years have been
Since then, I can hear mother ask,
"Are all the children in?"

I wonder if when the shadows fall
On the last short, earthly day,
When we say good-by to the world out-
side
All tired with our childish play,
When we step out into that other land
Where mother so long has been,
Will we hear her ask, just as of old,
"Are all the children in?"

A MOTHER'S PRAYER

A mother needs Thee, Lord,
So often through the day
For tiny, mischief-making hands,
For little feet that play.

A mother needs Thee, Lord,
Especially at night,
To fill the darkened corners with
Thy steady, quenchless light.

As once in Galilee,
So by the sick one's bed,
Bless every anxious mother's heart
As well as each small head.

Who taught my heart to seek,
My stubborn knee to bow,
Trusted to me these little ones;
I need Thee greatly — now.

Jeanette Saxton Coon

TO WHOM SHALL THEY GO?

O African mother, so full of fear,
To whom do you turn when the dark
valley is near?
To whom do you pour out your troubles
and cares?
You've no Saviour to cling to, no one
who shares.
Your pain and your woe! Oh! to whom
do you go?

O mother of India, so poor and so frail,
You turn to your idols to no avail.
You've no one to comfort you or no one
to bear
Your burdens and heartaches that I know
are there.
You've no loving Father on whom you
can cast
Every trial and problem and find rest
at last.

O mother of China, with sad aching heart,
To whom do you go to help take your
part?
You've no doctor or nurse to whom you
can phone.
You must bear the burdens of life all
alone.
O turn to my Saviour for freedom from
fear.
No matter what your problem, He will
always be near.

O heavenly Father, look down from
above.
Have pity on poor mothers, please show
them Thy love.
Show them Thy Son who died for their
sin.
Show them the new life they can have
within.

How they need Thee, as all of us do.
O, help many of them to come unto You.

AT MY MOTHER'S KNEE

I have worshipped in churches and
chapels,
I have prayed in the busy street;
I have sought my God and found Him
Where the waves of the ocean beat;
I have knelt in the silent forest,
In the shade of some ancient tree,
But the dearest of all my altars
Was raised at my *mother's knee*.

I have listened to God in His temple
I have caught His voice in the crowd;
I have heard Him speak when the
breakers
Were booming long and loud;
When the winds play soft in the treetops,
My Father has talked to me;
But I never have heard Him clearer
Than I did at my *mother's knee*.

The things in my life that are worthy
Were born in my mother's breast;
And breathed into mine by the magic
Of the love her life expressed.
The years that have brought me to man-
hood
Have taken her far from me;
But memory keeps me from straying
Too far from my *mother's knee*.

God, make me the man of her vision,
And purge me of all selfishness!
God, keep me true to her standards,
And help me to live to bless!
God, hallow the holy impress
Of the day that used to be,
And keep me a pilgrim forever
To the shrine at my *mother's knee*.

MOTHER

She always leaned to watch for us,
  Anxious if we were late,
In winter by the window,
  In summer by the gate.

And though we mocked tenderly,
  Who had such foolish care,
The long way home would seem more
    safe
Because she waited there.

Her thoughts were all so full of us,
  She never could forget!
And so I think that where she is
  She must be watching yet.

Waiting till we come home to her,
  Anxious if we were late —
Watching from heaven's window,
  Leaning o'er heaven's gate.

Margaret Widdemer

GOD'S IDEAL MOTHER

The mother who owns Christ as Lord
  And Saviour in her life;
The mother who has peace with God,
  Who has no inner strife;
The mother who knows how to trust
  The Father for all things;
The mother who is right and just,
  As punishment she brings.

The mother who knows how to pray
  For every daily need;
The mother who can point the way,
  Where God would have her lead;
The mother who knows how to guide
  A precious child to God;
The mother who walks by His side,
  Who walks the way He trod.

The mother who knows how to teach
  Her child the Holy Word;
The mother who knows how to reach
  A child who has not heard;
The mother who knows how to show
  A loving, tender face;
The mother who can help him grow
  In wisdom and in grace.

The mother who can make a home,
  In any place on earth;
The mother, who, though children roam,
  Has love that knows no dearth;
The mother who is all of this,
  To whom her God is real;
The mother who is not remiss,
  She is her God's ideal.

Cora M. Pinkham

MY MOTHER

They say the most of mothers
  Are something pretty fine,
But nobody else's mother
  Can be so dear as mine.

She never fails or falters
  When things go hard or wrong;
No matter what my troubles,
  She'll help me right along.

Her thought for me is endless —
  A million times a day
She gives me love and comfort,
  For which I cannot pay.

I can't begin to tell her
  My love in just a line,
But no one else's mother
  Is quite so dear as mine.

MY MOTHER'S LOVE

Her love is like an island
In life's ocean, vast and wide,
A peaceful, quiet shelter
From the wind, the rain, the tide,

'Tis bound on the North by hope,
By patience on the West,

By tender Counsel on the South
And on the East by rest.

Above it like a beacon light
Shine faith, and truth and prayer;
And through the changing scenes of life
I find a haven there.

New Year

THE GATES OF THE YEAR

The shadow gates are swinging
That hide the dawning year;
The sound of muffled ringing
Is swiftly growing clear;
The far-off music, falling
Like flutes soft and low,
Becomes a trumpet, calling,
And I must rise and go.

Lord, let my feet be surer
To walk the way unknown,
My heart a Kingdom purer,
With love upon its throne;
And let me have a vision
Of truth, and life, and need,
And hands of quick decision
For every noble deed.

And thus with humble gladness
I greet the dawning year,
With hope that conquers sadness,
And love that casts out fear;
With courage for my roaming
In mingled peace and strife,
Till some day, in the gloaming,
I find the gates of life.

John Mervin Hull

THE NEW YEAR

God gives to you another year,
A year of hours and days;
And as you face its unseen tasks
And face its unknown ways,
Lo! every hour some treasure holds,
And every day new joy unfolds.

A fragment of eternity
In which to gain and give;
So many days and weeks and months
To love and laugh and live.
What shall those minted moments buy?
How will you spend them as they fly?

They come all wrapped in silver morns,
That shade to golden noons,
Tied round with strings of jeweled stars,
Or sealed with mellow moons;
If one bring cloudy skies and rain,
A rainbow follows on its train.

So all that comes of seeming ill,
And all that you deem good
Are but God's precious thoughts of love
When rightly understood.
Another year all fresh and new
This is His loving gift to you.

93

THE NEW LEAF

He came to my desk with quivering lip;
The lesson was done.
"Have you a new leaf for me, dear
    Teacher?
I have spoiled this one!"
I took his leaf, all soiled and blotted,
And gave him a new one, all unspotted,
Then into his tired heart I smiled:
"Do better now, my child."

I went to the throne with trembling heart;
The year was done.
"Have you a new year for me, dear
    Master?
I have spoiled this one!"
He took my year, all soiled and blotted,
And gave me a new one, all unspotted,
Then into my tired heart He smiled:
"Do better now, my child!"

ANOTHER YEAR

Another year has now been born,
    The Old has died, the New is here,
We turn away from all the past,
    And face the future without fear.

Another year — Oh may it be
    A year unsullied, Lord, by sin?
The past we cannot alter now,
    But we the future still can win.

Another year to work and pray,
    To lead lost souls, dear Lord, to Thee;
Forgive us for our past mistakes,
    And make us all we long to be.

Another year to send the Light
    To those who have not heard Thy
    Name;
A year to welcome gain or loss,
    And humbly all Thy blessings claim.
                        Oswald J. Smith

RESOLUTIONS? —
NEW AND OLD

People all over at this time of year
    Are thinking back o'er the past
Regretting the failure of months gone by,
    Resolutions that did not last.
Intentions were good, resolutions fine,
    Every one well meant, indeed;
But most of the people who started out,
    All failed, they did not succeed.

We know that all are sick of the past,
    Desiring to be free
From the bondage of habits holding
    them —
    No victory can they see.
The same has been true year in and out,
    And repeated o'er and o'er;
'Till many have given up long ago,
    Refusing to try once more.

They know not the way laid down in
    God's Word,
    Wherein He says repent;
Begin wherein He says and do the first
    works,
    No longer His Word resent.
You've tried and you've failed, again and
    again,
    No power do you possess;
So, friend, it is time that you cease your
    way,
    Get down on your knees — confess.

When He has control of that life of yours,
    The failures of years gone by,
Will seem as nothing when Jesus takes
    o'er,
    And you have power from on high,
Oh yes, this New Year to you will be joy,
    All things to you will be new;
If only to Jesus you'll yield your all,
    He'll give His best unto you.
                        Harvey E. Rolfe

94

NEW YEAR'S WISHES

What shall I wish thee?
  Treasures of earth?
Songs in the springtime?
  Pleasure and mirth?
Flowers on the pathway?
  Skies ever clear?
Would this ensure thee
  A Happy New Year?

What shall I wish thee?
  What can be found
Bringing thee sunshine
  All the year round?
Where is the treasure,
  Lasting and dear,
That shall ensure thee
  A Happy New Year?

Faith that increaseth,
  Walking in light;
Hope that aboundeth,
  Happy and bright;
Love that is perfect,
  Casting out fear;
These shall ensure thee
  A Happy New Year.

Peace in the Saviour,
  Rest at His feet,
Smile of His countenance
  Radiant and sweet,
Joy in His presence!
  Christ ever near!
This will ensure thee
  A Happy New Year.

Frances Ridley Havergal

IF BUT ONE YEAR

If I had but one year to live;
  One year to help; one year to give;
One year to love; one year to bless;

One year of better things to stress;
One year to sing; one year to smile;
  To brighten earth a little while;
One year to sing my Master's praise;
  One year to fill with work my days;
When I should stand before my Lord,
  One year to strive for a reward
I think that I would spend each day,
  In just the very self-same way
The call may come to cross the bar
  Or raptured be to meet my Lord
At any time, and I must be
  Prepared to meet eternity.
So if I have a year to live,
  Or just one day in which to give
A pleasant smile, a helping hand,
  A mind that tries to understand
A fellow-creature when in need,
  'Tis one with me — I take to heed;
But try to live each day He sends
  To serve my gracious Master's ends.

MY NEW YEAR PRAYER

I hear the voice of the bells
  Announcing to the earth
Another year of frost and flower,
  Of promise, hope and birth.

Lord, teach me in the days to come,
  To do some worthy deed,
Guide some poor soul toward the light,
  Help some faint heart to succeed.

Let me not strive for self alone,
  But lend a hand to aid
The stranger on the upward path
  Who falters on the grade;

Strengthen my spirit that the weak
  At need may lean on me,
And make me, Lord, the instrument
  To lead their hearts to thee.

FORGET

Forget the old year's sorrows, forget its
lonely days,
Forget its toils and hardships, its dark
and weary ways;
Brood not o'er blighted prospects, o'er
hours with sadness rife —
Look forward to the new year, its hope,
its cheer, its life.

A gracious boon this new year, unsoiled
by sin or care;
No gem of earth so precious, no spring
time morn more fair:
Its worth can ne'er be measured, its
charms can ne'er be told;
But free, how free this new year, alike
to young and old.

How shall I spend this new year? The
answer's quickly given;
"Make each succeeding moment a step-
pingstone toward heaven;
Reach out thy hand in blessing to
suff'ring ones below;
'Twill keep thy cruse from failing,
and cause thy heart to glow.

"Send portions to the needy, go share
another's grief,
Point upward to the Master, who offers
sweet relief;
Sound out the gospel message, win lost
ones to the fold —
Thus spent, the joys of new year on earth
can ne'er be told."

A WISH FOR THE NEW YEAR

Health enough to make work a pleasure;
wealth enough to support your needs;
Strength enough to battle with difficulties
and overcome them;

Grace enough to confess your sins and
forsake them;
Patience enough to toil until some good
is accomplished;
Charity that shall see some good in your
neighbor;
Cheerfulness that shall make others glad;
Love that shall move you to be useful
and helpful;
Faith that shall make real the things of
God;
And *hope* that shall remove all anxious
fears concerning the future.
It is not doing the things we like to do,
but liking the things we have to do
That makes life blessed.

Phillips Brooks

RESOLVED

Resolved this year to better be,
And hoping that I can
Check up each day, and find that I
Have been a better man.

Resolved to cast away the frown
That never was worth while
And in its place, light up my face,
By putting on a smile.

Resolved to show more kindness
And regard mankind as brothers
Turn selfishness to helpfulness,
And try to live for others.

And now I pray Thy help, Dear Lord,
With it, I know I can
Be able every day to live
And be a better man.

Ottis Shirk

A PARABLE

Unknown to all except a few,
Between the Old Year and the New,
There is a little span of time,
No longer than the midnight's chime,
When two men meet, so I am told,
And one is young and the one is old.

The old man tells what he has thought;
The young man tells what he has brought.
If I could hear the words they say,
There soon would dawn a better day.
But I ring bells to greet the year,
And I blow horns — and I can't hear.

George L. Kress

I BURIED THE YEAR

I buried the year with its fellows,
The year I had loved so well;
  I buried it deep,
    Where the other years sleep;
I laid it to rest where it fell.

I buried the year with its sorrows;
'Tis well to forget the ill;
  I buried its tears,
    Its sins and its fears,
Its follies, its wrong, its ill will.

I buried the year, and above it
Erected a cross, to recall
  The Saviour who died,
    And the sin-cleansing tide,
Atoning and covering all.

I buried the year, but, on turning,
I found a new offspring of time
  Was born at my feet,
    And, with innocence sweet,
Was ready my old knees to climb.

I took the new year with rejoicing,
And ask for the grace and the love
  To train it aright
    For the kingdom of light,
The home in the heavens above.

W. Luff

ANOTHER YEAR

Another year is dawning!
  Dear Master, let it be,
In working or in waiting,
  Another year with Thee.

Another year of leaning
  Upon Thy loving breast,
Another year of trusting,
  Of quiet, happy rest.

Another year of mercies,
  Of faithfulness and grace;
Another year of gladness
  In the shining of Thy face.

Another year of progress
  Another year of praise;
Another year of proving
  Thy presence all the days.

Another year of service,
  Of witness for Thy love;
Another year of training
  For holier work above.

Another year is dawning,
  Dear Master, let it be,
On earth, or else in heaven,
  Another year for Thee!

F. R. Havergal

97

Others

COULD WE

Could we only see the goodness
  Of the ones we meet each day,
We'd not stop to criticize them
  As we pass along life's way.
We'd tell others of their merits,
  Rather than of faults we see;
Could we only see the goodness
  Much more pleasant it would be.
Could we only see the burden
  Carried by our fellowman,
We would be less prone to taunt him
  As this earthly sphere we span.
We would seek to aid our brother,
  Could we see the load he bears;
Critics would be few and scattered
  If we knew each other's cares:
Could we lift the misty curtain
  Veiling those we chance to meet,
We would be more kind and gentle
  To the travelers on life's street.
We would pluck the thorns that hurt
    them
  On the great highway of life,
Make it easier for the traveler,
  In this world where sin is rife.
Could we look into the future,
  See those lost eternally;
We'd bestir our souls from slumber,
  Cry to God incessantly.
We'd not loiter on the highway
  As we plod life's dusty road;
But we'd hasten to the rescue
  Of those souls near death's abode.

OTHERS

Let me remember on this day
That all I do or think or say
Will in some wondrous, magic way
Bring help or harm to others.

May my deeds be those of friendly cheer
Which bring a smile or dry a tear,
Give comfort and dispel a fear
Within the hearts of others.

In every thought may I pursue
A path both cleanly straight and true,
And find some star within the blue,
To which I may lead others.

FORBEARANCE

Instead of being sad and hurt
  By those who are unkind,
How better far it is to choose
  The opposite, and find
The way to peace and happiness
  Is graciously to do
To others as the Master taught
  You'd have them do to you.

True courtesy and gentleness
  Reveal an inward grace
That gives a glowing radiance,
  Transforms the plainest face.
Be calm, dear heart, and when oppressed
  Bless those who do you wrong,
And in forbearance love will prove
  There is no force so strong.

Della Adams Leitner

IF ONLY WE UNDERSTOOD

Could we but draw back the curtains
  That surround each other's lives,
See the naked heart and spirit,
  Know what spur the action gives,
Often we should find it better
  Purer than we judged we should,
We should love each other better,
  If we only understood.
If we knew the cares and trials,
  Knew the efforts all in vain,
And the bitter disappointment,
  Understood the loss and gain —

Would the grim, eternal roughness
  Seem — I wonder — just the same?
Should we help where now we hinder?
  Should we pity where we blame?
Ah, we judge each other harshly,
  Know not life's hidden force:
Knowing not the fount of action
  Is less turbid at its source:
Seeing amid the evil
  All the golden grain of good:
And we'd love each other better.
  If we only understood.

ON WITH THE MESSAGE

On with the Message! On with the Light!
On to the regions still shrouded in night,
On to the nations which never have
  heard;
On with the life-giving soul-saving
  Word.

On with the Message! Message of Pow'r.
Message to meet ev'ry need of the hour.
On with the Message o'er land and o'er
  sea;
On with the Truth that can set sinners
  free.

On with the Message! Carry it on.
Millions in darkness still pray for the
  dawn.
Millions for whom Christ's own blood
  did atone
Die in their darkness, unreached and
  alone.

On with the Message! Haste thee away;
Soon cometh night, haste thee on while
  'tis day
On with the Message, by love's passion
  stirred
On, till each creature of Jesus has heard.

On with the Message! Strive more and
  more,
Soon will the days for proclaiming be
  o'er.
On to all lengths, to where none have
  yet gone —
On with the Message! On, on, and on!

        Wesley Duewel

A LITTLE WORD

You'd be surprised, I'm sure, to know
How far a little word can go.
How many miles it runs away,
Up hill and down, in a single day;
How many angry hearts it wakes,
How many pleasant friends it makes;
What very wise things it can tell,
What very simple ones, as well;
How very busy, brave, and true,
How very false and lazy, too.
So take good care before that word
By anybody else is heard,
That it shall truly worthy be
To join a happy company
Of helpful words, that march with grace
And bear sweet sunshine in the face.

A HELPING HAND

If your brother has a burden
　Why not lend a helping hand?
Maybe you're the one God's chosen —
　Share his load and help him stand.

Have you ever had a problem?
　Felt a handclasp warm and true?
Did you feel the power of prayer
　From someone who cared for you?

Then I'm sure you will be ready
　With a kindly deed or two
When you see a needy brother
　For there's much that you can do.

You will never know the blessing
　That your acts of kindness brought,
Nor the faith you helped to strengthen
　When his aid through prayer you
　　sought.

So when God calls each one of us
　To show Christlike love again,
Let's work with willing hands and be
　Like the Good Samaritan.

God tells us in His Word that we
　Should comfort one another,
And if we really care enough
　We'll stop to help our brother.
Georgia B. Adams

PASS IT ON!

When the Saviour has given you a bless-
　ing, by paper or a book,
Do not leave it idly lying, in some soon
　forgotten nook.
There are others to be watered, and
　hungry souls to feed,
So seek to spread the blessing, that has

reached you in your need.
With its freshness yet upon you, 'ere the
　first glad glow has gone;
Let your heart look up for guidance, that
　your hand may pass it on.
And the one from you receiving, blessing
　gaining, just like you,
Can keep the blessing flowing, and pass
　it on anew
And when the day declares it, and you
　hear the words, "Well done,"
How sweet to know the Saviour was
　pleased — to see you *pass it on!*

FIRST TO THROW A STONE

If there's one who often falters
　By the wayside in despair,
Seems unusual his shortcomings,
　Do you hold him up in *prayer?*
If the weak should stumble, brethren,
　If he cannot stand alone,
Let the *perfect* one among you
　Be the first to throw a stone.

If so often he has wavered,
　You cannot believe him true,
Have you mentioned it to Jesus
　As the strong one ought to do?
Do you ever stop, consider?
　Have you no faults of your own?
Let the *perfect* one among you
　Be the first to throw a stone.

Is there one with crosses heavy,
　Seems he cannot carry all?
And he won't keep step as we do
　If he ever chance to fall,
Do you plead with God for mercy
　Till He answers from the throne?
Let the *perfect* one among you
　Be the first to throw a stone.

100

THE OTHER PERSON'S PLACE

Have you ever tried to get along
With someone whom you felt was wrong
In attitude and thought and speech;
Whose fellowship you could not reach?

Have you ever been misunderstood
Believing that your aims were good
By one who simply would not see
Your views, or with your words agree?

And has it also seemed that you,
If in his place, would try to do
In word and thought and deed the thing
That to yourself would comfort bring?

Then, having changed the parts around
And looking further, have you found
In accents of great clarity
A striking similarity?

How simple, then, the fault became
To understand, instead of blame;
What kindness, sympathy and grace
Lie in the other person's place!

Donald H. Hover

THE GOLDEN RULE

In your daily round of duties,
    As you make your way through life;
As you gaze upon its beauties,
    And you look upon its strife,
There's a rule of conduct given,
    Which I will commend to you:
Always do unto another
    What you'd have him do to you.

If, perchance, along life's highways,
    You should meet a man that's down,
Or you meet him on the byways,
    Where he meets with many a frown,

Won't you try to help him, brother,
    'Ere he passes from your view?
Won't you do unto another
    What you'd have him do to you?

Once upon a time the Saviour
    Came into this world of sin,
Came into this world to suffer,
    Precious souls that He might win.
And He gave to us a precept
    Did this Saviour, kind and true:
Always do unto another
    What you'd have him do to you.

James Wells

A CREED

Let me be a little kinder,
Let me be a little blinder
To the faults of those about me;
Let me praise a little more;
Let me be, when I am weary,
Just a little bit more cheery;
Let me serve a little better
To those that I am striving for.

Let me be a little braver
When temptation bids me waver;
Let me strive a little harder
To be all that I should be;
Let me be a little meeker
With the brother who is weaker;
Let me think more of my neighbor
And a little less of me.

Let me be a little sweeter,
Make my life a bit completer,
By doing what I should do
Every minute of the day;
Let me toil without complaining,
Not a humble task disdaining;
Let me face the summons calmly
When Death beckons me away.

101

GOD PITY HIM

God pity him who lives for self —
That one who does not share
The griefs and joys of other men,
That one who does not care.

God pity him who does not give
To others when in need;
God pity him who works and plans
For only selfish greed.

God pity him when sorrow comes
And no kind friend is there,
No one to grasp his trembling hand
And whisper low, "I care!"

God pity him when death shall come
And few stand by his bier;
So little missed by those he left,
They scarcely shed a tear!

God pity him who lives for self,
When the Master he shall see,
And Jesus says, "As you've done to them,
You've done it unto me."

THE DOWN-PULLERS

I never like the fellow's plan
  Who seeks to pull another down,
And laughs when he has caught his man
  And maybe takes away his crown;
Or would remove it if he could
  Although the fellow may be right;
Or if he's wrong, it's never good
  To hurt one with a greater blight.

The better plan for all, we know,
  Is lift the fallen to his feet;
Or if one's up, don't scheme to throw
  Across his path for him to meet
A stumbling stone, a rope or chain

You think may cause a mighty fall;
For by such plans you'll never gain
  The height of one who should be tall.
Walter E. Isenhour

"WHERE LOVE, THERE'S HEAVEN"

Where love, there's heaven and the home
So blest, there none will wish to roam;
Where Christian kindness and mirth
Prevail, there's joy and peace on earth.

When loving hearts forgive the pain
And hurt of little things, they gain
In peace and wisdom through the years;
Where love, there's joy amidst the tears.

No worldly gossip, vice or strife
Can ever build the better life
And he who hates must learn to love
And look within and look above.

Where love, there's heaven and the home
So blest, there none will wish to roam.
Mary Jacobs

LITTLE THINGS

God has no end of material
  For poets, priests and kings;
But what He needs is volunteers
  To do the *little* things.
There are many men who're ready
  To lead in battle and in strife;
But very few are willing to do
  The *little* things of life.
The widow's mite was a little thing
  From a money point of view;
But He who reads our inmost hearts,
  Sees more than mortals do.
Great deeds receive rewards below,
  And earth's applause is given;
But *little* things are seen by God
  From His watchtower in heaven.

Pastor

LET YOUR PASTOR KNOW

Mrs. Huff is up a miff tree
On a seat fixed good and firm,
And she'd like to tell the pastor
A few things to make him squirm.

Mrs. Huff was sick abed, sir,
Yes, sir, sick abed a week;
And the pastor didn't call, sir,
Not even took a peek.

Wasn't that enough, enough, sir
To provoke a saint to wrath?
And to make a Christian pilgrim
Wander from the churchly path?

When I asked her if the doctor
Called to see her, she said, "Sure"
And she looked as if she thought I
Needed some good strong mind cure.

Then I asked her how the doctor knew
That sickness laid her low,
And she said that she had called him
On the phone and told him so.

So the doctor called to see her,
But the pastor didn't go,
For the doctor knew that she was ill
And the pastor didn't know.

Now the doctor gets his bill paid
With a nicely written check,
But the pastor — for not knowing,
Simply "gets it in the neck."

SOFT JOB

The preacher works from morn till night
On one thing or the other.
He must be skilled at every trade
Or he just don't have it, brother.

He heals the sick, makes strong the weak;
He's carpenter and plumber.
When called to settle family rows,
He's wise and just acts dumber.

He's financier, he's architect,
Electrician, painter, teacher.
Of all these he must do well,
If he succeeds as "preacher."

His social habits must be good.
His job he never shirks.
In cold or heat, in rain or shine,
He's smiling as he works.

He goes from early morn till night,
In fact he's never done.
He often sees the rise and fall
Of both the moon and sun.

Whatever else has been left out,
He often does that too;
For thoughtless people never seem
To know when he is through.

He teaches, preaches, prays and talks,
And tries his best to win,
To Jesus Christ our Lord, and God,
The hearts and souls of men.

William C. Summers

103

THE PASTOR'S FRIEND

"The Church is dead," said brother
  Brown;
"It's true," said Gossip. "It's sure going
  down."
"I'm gonna quit," brother Gad-about
  'lowed,
"And go where there is a much bigger
  crowd."
Sister Selfish, too, was sure she could
  see —
"Not a soul in church 'preciates me."
Said brother Grumble, "I don't see why
The Sunday school's dead and the meet-
  ing's dry."
But good brother Faithful sat in his
  place;
The sunshine of heaven abeamin' on his
  face;
The good saint worshiped in prayer and
  song;
And to him — *there wasn't a single thing
  wrong!*

Whenever groups are called to meet,
  Her presence must be there;
And yet the members all agree
  She should live a life of prayer.

Though hearing people's burdens,
  Their griefs both night and day,
She ought to spread but sunshine
  To those along the way.

She must lend a sympathetic ear
  To every tale of woe,
Then forget about it
  Lest it to others go.

Her children must be models rare
  Of quietness and poise,
And still stay on the level
  With the other girls and boys.

You may think it quite an easy task,
  And just a pleasant life,
But really, it takes a lot of grace
  To be a preacher's wife.

THE PREACHER'S WIFE

You may think it quite an easy task,
  And just a pleasant life,
But really, it takes a lot of grace
  To be a preacher's wife.

She's supposed to be a paragon,
  Without a fault in view;
A saint when in the parsonage
  As well as in the pew.

Her home must be a small hotel
  For folks that chance to roam,
And yet have peace and harmony —
  The perfect preacher's home.

ATTENDING CHURCH

Attend church? Of course we do,
  Like others in our set,
Except on days that seem too cold
  Or hot or wet.
And then, of course, in summer,
  Just to keep up to par,
We take the kids on Sundays
  For a joy ride in the car.
And sometimes, too, in spring and fall
  I take a Sunday off
And hurry to the country club
  To have a game of golf.
But all the other Sundays
  You will find us in our pew,
For we always go to church
  When we've nothing else to do.

A PREACHER'S PRAYER

I do not ask
That crowds may throng the temple,
That standing room be at a price;
I only ask that, as I voice the message,
They may see Christ.

I do not ask
For churchly pomp, or pageant,
Or music such as wealth alone can buy;
I only ask that, as I voice the message,
He may be nigh.

I do not ask
That man may sound my praises,
Or headlines spread my name abroad;
I only ask that as I voice the message,
Hearts may find God.

I do not ask
For earthly place or laurel,
Of this world's distinction any part:
I only ask, when I voice the message
My Saviour's heart.

SOME BIRD

When the church seeks a pastor
  They often want
The strength of an eagle,
  The grace of a swan,
The gentleness of a dove,
  The friendliness of a sparrow,
And when they catch that bird
  They expect him to live
On the food of a canary.

THE PASTOR

He stood in the pulpit,
  So straight and so tall;
Expounding the truth,
  He seemed to know all.
The light on his face
  Was bright as the sun;
It was easy to see
  What the Saviour had done.
The chapel was silent,
  Except for his voice,
But as he proceeded,
  Many hearts did rejoice.
For the Master was speaking,
  Through His servant that day;
And at the conclusion,
  They rejoiced on their way.

William C. Summers

STAND BY

The preacher does better
  When you are there;
'Tis hard to preach
  To an empty chair.
But your chair is not empty
  When you're away,
For Satan's imps
  Are there that day!

They make faces
  At the preacher's text.
And show the folks
  Who are sitting next.
And show them how much
  The church is down
And it is all because
  You're out of town.

Prayer

MY PRAYER

I asked the Lord that I might grow
  In faith, and love and grace,
Might more of His salvation know,
  And seek more earnestly His face.

'Twas He who taught me thus to pray,
  And He, I trust, has answered prayer,
But it has been in such a way
  As almost drove me to despair.

I hoped that in some favored hour,
  At once He'd answer my request,
And by His love's constraining power,
  Subdue my sins and give me rest.

Instead of this, He made me feel
  The hidden evils of my heart,
And let the angry powers of hell
  Assault my soul in every part.

Yes, more, with His own hand He
    seemed,
  Intent to aggravate my woe,
Cross all the fair designs I schemed,
  Blasted my gourds and laid me low.

"Lord, why is this?" I trembling cried,
  "Wilt Thou pursue Thy worm to
    death?"
" 'Tis in this way," the Lord replied,
  "I answer prayer for grace and faith.

"These inward trials I employ,
  From self and pride to set thee free,
And break thy schemes of earthly joy,
  That thou may'st seek thine all in Me."

106

TRAVELING ON MY KNEES

Last night I took a journey
  To a land far 'cross the seas;
I didn't go by boat or plane,
  I traveled on my knees.

I saw so many people there
  In deepest depths of sin,
And Jesus told me I should go,
  That there were souls to win.

But I said, "Jesus, I can't go
  And work with such as these."
He answered quickly, "Yes, you can
  By traveling on your knees."

He said, "You pray; I'll meet the need,
  You call and I will hear;
Be concerned about lost souls,
  Of those both far and near."

And so I tried it, knelt in prayer,
  Gave up some hours of ease;
I felt the Lord right by my side
  While traveling on my knees.

As I prayed on and saw souls saved
  And twisted bodies healed,
And saw God's workers' strength renewed
  While laboring on the field,

I said, "Yes, Lord, I have a job,
  My desire Thy will to please;
I can go and heed Thy call
  By traveling on my knees."

Sandra Goodwin

PRAY, CHRISTIAN, PRAY!

If you want a great revival
From South to Arctic Pole,
If you want the blood of Jesus
To make the sin-sick whole,
If you want to see God's kingdom
Come in with mighty power,
If you want to see our nation
A strong and righteous power,
Then pray, Christian, pray!

If you want to hear your pastor
Preach fervently with love,
If you want to win lost sinners
To Christ and "Home" above,
If you want the Holy Spirit
To teach you of true worth,
If you want to see the glory
Of God upon this earth,
Then pray, Christian, pray!

If you want the sparkling waters
To flood your thirsty soul,
If you want to see religion
In tidal waves that roll,
If you want to send the Gospel
To continents afar,
If you want to see an ending
To ghastly, bloody war,
Then pray, Christian, pray!

If you want to follow Jesus
And honor His dear Name,
If you want the fire enkindled
Into a holy flame,
If you ever hope to finish
The task you have begun,
If you want the loving Father
To say to you, "Well done,"
Then pray, Christian, pray!

PRAYER

Prayer must be grounded on the Word
Accompanied with faith
Thus, what's according to His will
God answers — as He saith.

God never fails to answer prayer
In fervency implored;
So, let each need presented be
Before our gracious Lord.

If these conditions be fulfilled
God's blessing will impart
Fulness of joy, and faith, and love
To every waiting heart.

A DRIVER'S PRAYER

Dear Lord — before I take my place
Today behind the wheel,
Please let me come with humble heart
Before Thy throne to kneel
And pray, that I am fit to drive
Each busy thoroughfare,
And that I keep a watchful eye
Lest some small child be there.

And keep me thinking constantly
About the Golden Rule
When driving past the playground zone
Or by some busy school
Then when I stop to give someone
His right to cross the street,
Let me, my brother's keeper be
And spare a life that's sweet.

Please make me feel this car I drive
You gave me to enjoy,
And that its purpose is to serve
Mankind, but not destroy.

PRAY!

Pray in the early morning
　For grace throughout the day;
We know not what temptations
　And trials may cross our way.

Pray in the gladsome noontide,
　When the day is at its best;
Pray when the night o'ertakes thee
　To Him who giveth rest.

Pray in the silent midnight,
　If wakeful hours be thine;
Pray for a heart submissive,
　That never will repine.

Pray in the hour of sorrow,
　Pray in the hour of grief;
In coming to the Father,
　Thy soul shall find relief.

Pray when the sun shines brightest,
　Thy path with roses strewn;
Pray that thy heart be ever
　With the Saviour's kept in tune.

Pray when the dark day cometh,
　And clouds hang overhead;
In the secret of His presence
　Thy soul hath naught to dread.

Pray for the Father's guidance
　In all thy works and ways,
So shall thy days be fruitful,
　Thy life be full of praise.

Living in touch with Jesus,
　Keeping our own hearts right,
Others will be attracted
　From darkness into light.

Mrs. Major Arnold

A PRAYER

*(Found in the Chester Cathedral
in the eighteenth century)*

Give us a good digestion, Lord,
　And also something to digest.
Give us a healthy body, Lord,
　With sense to keep it at its best.
Give us a healthy mind, good Lord,
　To keep the good and pure in sight,
Which seeing sin is not appalled,
　But finds a way to set it right.
Give us a mind that is not bored,
　That does not whimper, whine or sigh;
Don't let us worry over much
　About the fussy thing called "I."
Give us a sense of humor, Lord;
　Give us the grace to see a joke,
To get some happiness from life,
　And pass it on to other folk.　Amen.

DO I REALLY PRAY?

I often say my prayers,
　But do I really pray?
And do the wishes of my heart
　Go with the words I say?

I may as well kneel down
　And worship gods of stone,
As offer to the living God
　A prayer of words alone.

For words without the heart
　The Lord will never hear;
Nor will He to those lips attend
　Whose prayer is not sincere!

Lord, show me what I need
　And teach me how to pray,
And help me when I seek Thy grace
　To mean the words I say.

John Burton

AN INTERCESSOR

Make me an Intercessor,
  One who can really pray,
One of the Lord's remembrancers,
  By night as well as day.

Make me an Intercessor,
  Through whom the spirit can plead,
For the sin and sorrow on ever side
  Of this world in darkness and need.

Make me an Intercessor,
  In spirit-touch with Thee,
And given the Heavenly vision,
  Pray through to victory.

Make me an Intercessor,
  Teach me how to prevail,
To stand my ground and still pray on,
  Though powers of hell assail.

Make me an Intercessor,
  'Til pleading at Thy Throne,
The sins and sorrows of other lives
  Become as my very own.

Make me an Intercessor,
  Sharing Thy Death and life,
In prayer claiming for others
  Victory in the strife.

Make me an Intercessor,
  Willing for deeper death,
Emptied, broken, then made anew,
  And filled with Living Breath.

Make me an Intercessor,
  Hidden — unknown — set apart,
Thought little of by those around,
  But satisfying Thine Heart.

WHAT IS PRAYER?

Prayer is the soul's sincere desire,
  Uttered or unexpressed;
The motion of a hidden fire
  That trembles in the breast.

Prayer is the burden of a sigh,
  The falling of a tear,
The upward glancing of an eye,
  When none but God is near.

Prayer is the simplest form of speech
  That infant lips can try;
Prayer the sublimest strains that reach
  The Majesty on high.

Prayer is the contrite sinner's voice,
  Returning from his ways;
While angels in their songs rejoice
  And cry, "Behold, he prays!"

Robertson

A FATHER'S PRAYER

Dear God, my little boy of three
Has said his nightly prayer to Thee;
Before his eyes were closed in sleep
He asked that Thou his soul would keep;
And I, still kneeling at his bed,
My hand upon his tousled head,
Do ask, with deep humility,
That Thou, dear Lord, remember me.
Make me, kind Lord, a worthy dad,
That I may lead this little lad
In pathways ever fair and bright,
That I may keep his steps aright.
O God, his trust must never be
Destroyed or even marred by me.
So for the simple things he prayed
With childish voice so unafraid,
I, trembling, ask the same from Thee;
Dear Lord, kind Lord, remember me.

Chicago Daily Tribune
in Moody Monthly

109

MORE PRAYER

"More ships!" some cry; "more guns!"
    "More fighters in the air!"
But, wise the king who adds,
    "More prayer!"

Remember, angels use
    This ancient thoroughfare;
So keep their highway clear —
    More prayer!

One day will not suffice
    To meet time's wear and tear,
Each hour of life must see
    More prayer!

Again and yet again,
    The scrolls of God declare:
"The deepest need of men —
    "More prayer!"

THE HOUR OF PRAYER

Oh, what precious peace I find
    In the hour of prayer —
When my Father's gentle touch
    Scatters every care!

'Tis the only place I know;
    'Tis a blest retreat
Where my soul contentment finds
    At His mercy seat.

He will hear at any time,
    He knows what I'll say
For He knows my inmost thoughts
    Long before I pray!

Oh, what precious peace I find
    In the hour of prayer,
'Tis the only place I know
    Have you met Him there?

Georgia B. Adams

BE STILL, MY HEART

Not so in haste, my heart
Have faith in God, and wait;
Although He lingers long,
He never is too late.

Until He cometh, rest,
Nor grudge the hours that roll,
The feet that wait for God
Are soonest at the goal.

Are soonest at the goal.
That is not gained by speed,
Then hold thee still, my heart,
For I shall wait His lead.

WHO PRAYED?

Did you think of us this morning
    As you breathed a word of prayer?
Did you ask for strength to help us
    All our heavy burdens bear?

Did you speak of faith and courage
    For the trials we must meet?
Did you ask that God might keep us
    As you bowed at Jesus' feet?

Someone prayed, and strength was given
    For the long and weary road.
Someone prayed and faith grew stronger
    As we bent beneath our load.

Someone prayed—the way grew brighter,
    And we walked all unafraid.
In our heart a song of gladness —
    Tell us: Was it you who prayed?

A Missionary

THE SECRET PLACE

There is a place where thou canst touch
  the eyes
  Of blinded men to instant, perfect
  sight;

There is a place where thou canst say,
  "Arise!"
  To dying captives, bound in chains of
  night.

There is a place where thou canst reach
  the store
  Of hoarded gold, and free it for the
  Lord;

There is a place here, or on a distant
  shore,
  Where thou canst send the worker and
  the Word.

There is a place where heaven's resistless
  power
  Responsive moves to thine insistent
  plea;

There is a place, a silent holy hour,
  Where God Himself descends and
  works for thee.

Where is that secret place? — dost thou
  ask, "Where?"
  O soul, it is the secret place of prayer!
  A. A. Pollard

PRAY!

Pray! for earth has many a need.
Pray! for prayer is vital deed.
Pray! for God in heaven hears.
Pray! prayer will move the spheres.
Pray! for praying leads to peace.
Pray! for prayer gives release.
Pray! for prayer is never lost.
Pray! for prayer well pays its cost.
Pray! for prayer is always power.
Pray! for every prayer's a flower.
Pray! for prayer the Saviour finds.
Pray! for prayer creation binds.
Pray! for every prayer is gold.
Pray! for prayer is joy untold.
Pray! for praying frees from care.
Pray! for Jesus joins your prayer.
  Amos R. Wells

PRAYER MOVES THE HAND THAT MOVES THE WORLD

There is an eye that never sleeps
  Beneath the wing of the night;
There is an ear that never shuts
  When sink the beams of light.

There is an arm that never tires
  When human strength gives way;
There is a love that never fails
  When earthly loves decay.

That eye is fixed on seraph throngs;
  That arm upholds the sky;
That ear is filled with angel songs;
  That love is throned on high.

But there's a power which man can wield,
  When mortal aid is vain,
That eye, that arm, that love to reach,
  That listening ear to gain.

That power is prayer, which soars on
  high,
  Through Jesus, to the throne,
And moves the hand which moves the
  world,
  To bring salvation down.
  John A. Wallace

MY DAILY PRAYER

O Father, keep me through this day;
In Him who washed my sins away.

And guide me through the morrow, Thou;
Watch o'er me then, as even now.

O lead me truly by that One,
The Spirit of Thine only Son.

Keep me within His love and grace;
The Christ, the lovely, fair of face.

My Father, may I e'er for Thee
Thy witness, intercessor be.

Within the center of Thy will
Keep me, O Father, restful, still.

And by the power of Thy hand,
O compass me, as Thou hast planned.

And keep me 'neath Thy shelt'ring wings;
Away from sinful, earthly things.

My Father, keep me now, alway;
For 'tis in Jesus' name I pray. Amen.

Eva Gray

THE SECRET PLACE
OF PRAYER

I love the secret place of prayer,
The shining mercy seat;
My precious Lord is always there
And fellowship is sweet.

How blest a refuge when the way
Has seemed so hard to see,
How wonderful to hear Him say,
"Nothing's too hard for Me."

Alone with God in quietness,
Apart from earthly care,
I praise Him for the blessedness
Of every answered prayer.

My precious Lord invites me to
This privilege so rare —
That's why I love the secret place,
The secret place of prayer!

Georgia B. Adams

PRAY ON!

Pray on! Our God is on His throne.
Tell Him your every need;
The One who hears and answers prayer
Will to your cry give heed.

Pray on! Elijah's God still lives.
He bends to catch your prayer.
He'll never fail His trusting child;
Your griefs He'll surely bear.

Pray on! Our God will answer prayer;
His ears are quick to hear
He knows the anxious, troubled heart;
He sees your every tear.

Pray on! Fight on, be true;
Our God still loves His own.
Your faith, though small, He will reward;
He reigns upon His throne.

Pray on! The answer yet will come
Though seemingly delayed;
In spite of all the foe may do,
Fear not, be not dismayed.

One day 'ere long we'll cease to pray;
Our prayers shall turn to praise.
We then shall see Him face to face —
Oh, glorious day of days!

NO DOUBT

You may hear a pygmy talking
　Over the radio;
On a television program
　You may see the Antarctic snow;
You may hear the lovely music
　Of a distant violin,
And watch a child united
　With his long-imprisoned kin.
If you can see and hear such things
　That travel through the air,
How could you ever doubt that God
　Sees you and hears your prayer?

Helen Baker Adams

AND SO SHOULD YOU

The camel, at the close of day,
Kneels down upon the sandy plain
To have his burden lifted off
And rest again.

My soul, thou, too, shouldst to thy knees
When daylight draweth to a close,
And let thy Master lift the load
And give repose.

The camel kneels at morning's dawn
To have the guide replace his load —
Then rises up anew, to take
The desert road . . .

SECRET PRAYER

Go when the morning shineth,
　Go when the noon is bright,
Go when the eve declineth,
　Go in the hush of night:
Go with pure mind and feeling,
　Fling every fear away,
And in thy chamber kneeling,
　Go thou, in secret pray.

Remember all who love thee,
　And all who are loved by thee,
Pray, too, for those who hate thee,
　If any such there be:
Then, for thyself in meekness,
　A blessing humbly claim,
And link with each petition
　The great Redeemer's name.

Or if 'tis ever denied thee
　In solitude to pray,
Should holy thoughts come o'er thee
　When friends are round thy way,
E'en then the silent breathing
　Of thy spirit raised above,
May reach His throne of glory,
　Who is mercy, truth and love.

John Cross Belle

THE HOUR OF PRAYER

My God, is any hour so sweet,
　From blush of morn to evening star,
As that which calls me to Thy feet,
　The hour of prayer?

No words can tell what sweet relief
　Here for my every want I find;
What strength for warfare, balm for grief,
　What peace of mind.

Hushed is each doubt, gone every fear;
　My spirit seems in heaven to stay;
And e'en the penitential tear
　Is wiped away.

Lord, till I reach that blissful shore,
　No privilege so dear shall be,
As thus my inmost soul to pour
　In prayer to Thee.

Charlotte Elliott

SOMEBODY PRAYED

Somebody prayed, and refreshing rain
Fell on the parching grass and grain,
Cooling, reviving; the drought was stayed
And food was growing — for somebody
    prayed.

Somebody prayed, and a hospital grew,
With long, cool windows and lovely view,
With clean, white cots for fevered heads,
And white-capped nurses with gentle
    tread.

Somebody prayed, and peaceful rest
Sweetly came to the troubled breast,
Bringing new hope where anguish before
Crushed and darkened life's pathway o'er.

Somebody prayed, and across the sea
The old, old story of Calvary,
With its new, sweet meaning of love
    untold,
To the waiting millions' hearts was told.

Somebody prayed! Oh, gift divine!
Linked with service for yours and mine;
Communing each day with the living
    Lord,
Working and waiting to prove His Word.

PRAYER — ANSWER

At first I prayed for Light:
    Could I but see the way,
How gladly, swiftly would I walk
    To everlasting day!

And next I prayed for Strength
    That I might tread the road
With firm, unfaltering feet, and win
    To heaven's serene abode.

And then I asked for Faith:
    Could I but trust my God,

I'd live enfolded in His peace,
    Though fears were all abroad.

But now I pray for Love:
    Deep love to God and man;
A living love that will not fail,
    However dark the plan.

And Light, and Strength and Faith
    Are opening everywhere!
God only waited for me till
    I prayed the larger prayer.
                            Ednah D. Cheney

TAKE TIME TO TALK
WITH GOD

Take time to talk with God before you
    hurry
    To life's appointed tasks, Bring all your
    care,
Your disillusionment, your doubt, your
    worry,
    And talk it over with the Lord in
    prayer.

Take time to talk with God. He stands
    between you
    And all the unexpected that can come;
From every unseen foe His love would
    screen you,
    And in its warmth are light and peace
    and home.

Take time to talk with God. Be not
    contriving
    To push beyond today's uncertain rim,
Commit it to the Lord, Not all our
    striving
    Can do as much as one small word with
    Him.
                        Helen Frazee-Bower

114

A PRAYER

Jesus, Thy life is mine!
  Dwell evermore in me;
And let me see
  That nothing can untwine
Thy life from mine.

Thy life in me be shown!
  Lord, I would henceforth seek
To think and speak
  Thy thoughts, Thy words alone,
No more my own.

Thy fullest gift, O Lord,
  Now at Thy word I claim
Through Thy dear Name
  And touch the rapturous chord
Of praise forth-poured.

Jesus, my life is Thine
  And ever more shall be
Hidden in Thee!
  For nothing can untwine
Thy life from mine.

WHEN NOBODY PRAYS

In a certain crypt-like courtroom,
A boy with tousled hair
Stood before a stern old judge,
A child of cold despair.
The youth explained his downfall
With this peculiar plea —
"Your honor," was his bitter sob,
"Nobody prayed for me."

"Next case!" the court clerk cried,
And a woman of the street
Was ushered from the dim-lit hall,
To face the judgment seat.
In the still and chilly chamber
Was heard her painful plea;

A scarlet siren's wistful words —
"Nobody prayed for me."

Now, next, before the cold old judge
A "drunk" was herded in,
And faced the scowling magistrate,
His body worn and thin.
"Well judge, I guess I'm guilty,"
Came the drunkard's candid plea:
"I can't give up drink, sir,
"Nobody prays for me."

                    Merl A. Clapper

BECAUSE YOU PRAYED

Because you prayed
God touched our weary bodies with His
  power,
And gave us strength for every trying
  hour
In which we might have faltered,
Had not, our intercessors,
Faithful been and true.

Because you prayed
God touched our lips with coals from
  altar fire,
Gave spirit fullness, and did so inspire
That when we spoke, sin-blinded souls
  did see;
Sin-chains were broken;
Captives were made free.

Because you prayed
The "Dwellers in the Dark" have found
  the light.
The glad, good news has banished
  heathen night.
The message of the cross so long delayed
Has brought them life at last.
Because you prayed.
                        C. B. B.

115

THE ANSWERED PRAYER

I prayed for strength, and then I lost
awhile
All sense of nearness, human and divine;
The love I leaned on, failed and pierced
my heart,
The hands I clung to loosed themselves
from mine;
And while I swayed, weak, trembling and
alone,
The everlasting arms upheld my own.

I prayed for light; the sun went down in
clouds,
The moon was darkened by my misty
doubt,
The stars of heaven were dimmed by
earthly fears
And all my little candle flame burned out;
But while I sat in shadow, wrapped in
night
The face of Christ made all the darkness
bright.

I prayed for peace, and dreamed of
restful ease,
A slumber drugged from pain, a hushed
repose;
Above my head the skies were black with
storm,
And fiercer grew the onslaught of my
foes;
But while the battle raged, and wild
winds blew
I heard His voice, and perfect peace I
knew.

I thank Thee, Lord, Thou art too kind
to heed
My feeble prayers, and answer as I
sought,

Since these rich gifts Thy bounty has
bestowed
Have brought me more than I have asked
or thought.
Giver of good, so answer each request
With Thine own giving, better than my
best.

Annie Johnson Flint

PRAYER ANSWERED

I asked for strength that I might achieve;
He made me weak that I might obey.
I asked for health that I might do greater
things;
I was given grace that I might do better
things.
I asked for riches that I might be happy;
I was given poverty that I might be wise.
I asked for power that I might have the
praise of men;
I was given weakness that I might feel
the need of God.
I asked for all things that I might enjoy
life;
I was given life that I might enjoy all
things.
I received nothing that I asked for, all
that I hoped for,
My prayer was answered.

A MORNING PRAYER

I ask Thee not to withhold grief
Thou hast in store for me;
I only ask for courage, Lord,
To bear it patiently.
Some day the azure sky will break,
And Thy dear face I'll see;
I pray that Thou wilt find me, Lord,
Waiting patiently.

Betty Perpetuo

PURER IN HEART

Purer in heart, O God,
　Help me to be;
May I devote my life
　Wholly to Thee
Watch Thou my wayward feet
　Guide me with counsel sweet;
Purer in heart, help me to be.

Purer in heart, O God,
　Help me to be;
Teach me to do Thy will
　Most lovingly.
Be Thou My Friend and Guide,
　Let me with Thee, abide
Purer in heart, help me to be.

Purer in heart, O God
　Help me to be;
That I Thy holy Face
　One day may see.
Keep me from secret sin,
　Reign Thou my soul within;
Purer in heart, help me to be.

PRAYER

I know not by what methods rare;
But this I know: God answers prayer.
I know that He has given His Word,
Which tells me prayer is always heard
And will be answered, soon or late;
And so I pray and calmly wait.

I know not if the blessing sought
Will come in just the way I thought,
But leave my prayer with Him alone
Whose will is wiser than my own,
Assured that He will grant my quest
Or send some answer far more blessed.

FLAME OF GOD

From prayer that asks that I may be
Sheltered from winds that beat on Thee,
From fearing when I should aspire,
From faltering when I should climb
　higher,
From silken self, O Captain free
Thy soldier who would follow Thee.

From easy choices, weakenings,
Not thus are spirits fortified,
Not this way went the Crucified,
From all that dims Thy Calvary,
O Lamb of God, deliver me.

Give me the love that leads the way,
The faith that nothing can dismay,
The hope no disappointments tire,
The passion that will burn like fire,
Let me not sink to be a clod:
Make me Thy fuel, Flame of God.

Amy Carmichael

BE STILL

I want to be still as a quiet hill,
　As mute as a silent rock,
And listen to things like cricket wings
　Or the tick of a little clock . . .

I want to glide on a sleeping tide
　Far out on a great calm sea
And dream of shores untouched by wars,
　Of peace that is yet to be . . .

I want to be part of the one great heart
　Of silent, celestial space,
And let time roll till I fill my soul
　With the light from the Master's face.

Betsy W. Kline

117

Salvation — Conversion

COME UNTO ME

"Come unto Me," said One below,
  "Come unto Me and rest.
My yoke is easy, burden light,
  My servants ever blest,
To weary souls and aching limbs
  I offer sweet release,
And lives by sin and sadness crushed
  In Me find perfect peace."

"To you I come," the Spirit saith,
  "To you bring light and cheer;
No longer dwells your Lord with men.
  But I am ever near;
I bring you truth, and strength, and
    grace;
  I draw from endless store,
And on the sacred record shine
  That you may love Him more."

"Come unto Me," says One above,
  "Come to your Father's home;
A rough and stormy way is yours
  The while on earth you roam.
But here for those who conquer sin
  Unfolded treasures lie,
And they who faithful serve below
  Shall rule with Me on high."

John Stuart

THE SOUL

What is the thing of greatest price,
The whole creation, round?
That which was lost in paradise;
That which in Christ is found.
The soul of man, Jehovah's breath;

It keeps two worlds in strife.
Hell works beneath its work of death,
Heaven stoops to give it life.

WHAT MUST I DO TO BE SAVED?

Nothing, either great or small,
  Nothing, sinner, no;
Jesus did it, did it all,
  Long, long ago.

When He from His lofty throne
  Stooped to do and die,
Everything was fully done;
  Hearken to His cry —

"It is finished!" Yes, indeed!
  Finished every jot.
Sinner, this is all you need;
  Tell me is it not?

Weary, working, burdened one,
  Wherefore toil you so?
Cease your doing; all was done
  Long, long ago.

Till to Jesus' work you cling,
  By a simple faith,
"Doing" is a deadly thing —
  "Doing" ends in death.

Cast your deadly "doing" down —
  Down at Jesus' feet;
Stand "in Him," in Him alone,
  Gloriously "complete!"

COME UNTO ME

Come unto Me, said Jesus,
  Ye who are weary and worn,
Bring unto Me your burdens,
  And hearts that are anguish torn.

Come unto Me, ye toilers,
  Tired of the stress and strife,
Find in Me a resting place,
  And calm for that troubled life.

Bring unto Me your sorrows,
  Ye who are bowed with grief,
I have a joy for those who mourn,
  And a peace that brings relief.

Come unto Me, ye restless,
  Homeless and friendless, O come,
And I will give you a resting place,
  A place in My Father's home.

I know what it means to be weary,
  With no place to lay My head,
I have shared the sorrows of many,
  And have wept beside their dead.

Then come unto Me, ye troubled,
  Ye who are sore distressed,
Come, and in coming to Me you find
  A sweet and perfect rest.

Flora Osgood

I NEVER KNEW

I never knew what real peace meant
  Until His peace He gave.
I never knew how lost I was
  Until He came to save.

I never knew how to forgive
  Until He pardoned me.

I never felt so clean within,
  Till I was malice free.

I never knew what real joy meant
  Until His joy I knew.
I never scaled the blessed heights
  Until Christ thrilled me through.

I never knew what real friends were
  Until His life touched mine.
I never knew a friend could be
  Like Him, my Friend divine.

Glenn E. Wagoner

THERE IS A PLACE

There is a place of peace and rest,
  'Tis at the Saviour's side;
It's there we find that quietness,
  That ever will abide.

There is a place where calm prevails,
  'Mid all the wars and strife;
It is in Jesus Christ, our Lord,
  Who hides us in His life.

There is a place of quietness,
  That calms our doubts and fears,
'Tis round the person of God's Son,
  Who drives away our tears.

There is a place of calm retreat,
  On Jesus' loving breast,
When tired and weary from the strain,
  'Tis there that we find sweet rest.

There is a place of happiness,
  And joy beyond compare;
'Tis in the center of God's will,
  May we abide just there.

Alma Hoellein

ROOM FOR JESUS

Have you any room for Jesus,
  Has He spoken to your heart?
Have you answered to His pleading,
  "Let Me all My grace impart"?

He will heal the sin-sick sinner,
  He will answer every plea;
Trust in Him for He will save you;
  From sin's grasp He'll set you free.

Trust Him now, O wait no longer;
  Now the day of grace is here;
Now salvation you may have, friend,
  If you'll trust Him, never fear.

He will save you, He will keep you
  From sin's fetters, fear and woe;
He will banish Satan's powers,
  And He'll conquer every foe!
            Barbara H. Staples

CHRIST, MY SALVATION

Christ, my Lord, is my salvation
  Him I'll trust, and never fear
When the tempter's darts assail me,
  And the tempest draweth near.

Christ, my strength, the Rock of Ages,
  Is my joy and perfect song;
To Him, fairest of ten thousands,
  Doth my heart and soul belong.

Him I will declare, yes, mention,
  As I cry and shout and sing
Of His wells of great salvation
  In my song I'll praises bring.

I will praise His name forever,
  Worship, love and Him adore;

In the ceaseless, endless ages
  Praise His name forevermore.
            Eva Gray

ON TIME WITH GOD

God has His times: No power of man
  Can thwart His purposes divine;
For everything He has a plan
  And one for this small life of mine.

I want to be on time with God,
  My footsteps guided in His ways;
His will and mine of one accord,
  My highest joy to speak His praise.

I want to be on time with God,
  Nor fail Him when He calls to me;
I'll follow Him at home, abroad
  'Til time becomes eternity.
            C. D. Nutter

TOO BUSY

Too busy this morning
  I'll say a prayer quick;
Tonight I'll have time
  To study and to think.

Tonight I'm too tired
  To study God's Word.
I'll wait 'til next week
  Then I'll worship the Lord.

Next week came too fast;
  But it seems that I may
Have more time next month
  To read and then to pray.

Next month! Oh, yes,
  I just wonder why
My love for the Lord
  Is about ready to die.

WHAT THEN?

When the great, busy plants of our cities
  Shall have turned out their last finished
    work;
When our merchants have sold their last
    order,
  And dismissed every hard-working
    clerk;
When our banks have all counted the last
  of their notes
  And paid out their last dividend:
When the Judge of the earth wants a
    hearing
  And asks for a balance — what then?

When the choir has sung its last anthem,
  And the preacher has voiced his last
    prayer;
When the people have heard their last
    sermon,
  And the sound has died out on the air;
When the Bible lies closed in the pulpit
  And the pews are all empty of men;
When we stand each one facing his
    record —
  And the great Book is opened — what
    then?

When the actors have played their last
    drama,
  And the mimic has made his last fun;
When the movie has flashed its last
    picture,
  And the billboard displayed its last
    run;
When the crowds seeking pleasure have
    vanished,
  And gone out into darkness again —
When the trumpet of ages has sounded—
  And we stand up before Him — what
    then?

SIN AND ITS CURE

The worst of all diseases
  Is light compared with sin;
On every part it seizes,
  But rages most within.

'Tis palsy, plague, and fever,
  And madness all combined;
And none but a believer
  The least relief can find.

From men great skill professing
  I thought a cure to gain,
But this proved more distressing,
  And added to my pain.

Some said that nothing ailed me,
  Some gave me up for lost;
Thus every refuge failed me,
  And all my hopes were crossed.

At length the Great Physician,
  How matchless is His grace,
Accepted my petition,
  And undertook my case.

First gave me sight to view Him,
  For sin my eyes had sealed,
Then bid me look unto Him;
  I looked, and I was healed!

TRANSFORMED

I asked the roses as they grew
Richer and lovelier in hue,
What made their tints so rich and bright?
They answered, "Looking toward the
    light."
Ah, secret dear, said heart of mine,
God meant my life to be like thine,
Radiant with heavenly beauty bright,
By simply looking toward the light.
            D. Weston Gates

I CAME TO JESUS

I came to Jesus as I was,
  Unlearned and unwise;
He took me as He only does,
  And healed my blinded eyes,
I saw the glory of His Word,
  From me went all my fears;
His gentle voice my spirit heard,
  When dried were all my tears.

I came to Jesus with my sin,
  Sufficient was His grace;
And now He sweetly dwells within
  'Tis His abiding place,
The joy of my salvaiton, He,
  My perfect righteousness;
'Tis He alone that comforts me,
  My soul He now doth bless.

I came to Jesus with my guilt,
  From it I was released;
Through His dear blood that once was
    spilt,
  My sorrow's quickly ceased,
The anguish in my heart was stilled,
  I felt a joy divine;
With His own grace my soul He filled,
  And made my face to shine.

I came to Jesus as a child,
  In sin no more to roam;
In love upon my face He smiled,
  And gave to me a home.
Sweet, happy fellowship have we,
  My gracious Lord and I;
From sin and shame He sets me free,
  And guides me with His eye.

I came, I came to Jesus Christ,
  'Twas He who saved my soul,
'Twas He who washed me in His blood,
  And made my spirit whole.

He is the sunshine of my heart,
  My happy resting place.
Glad am I that I came to Him.
  And found His truth and grace.
                    George White

WILL GOD'S PATIENCE HOLD OUT FOR YOU?

The patience of Job is a story old,
  We marvel at this good man.
Yet infinitely greater God's patience is
  Toward those who reject His plan.
He yearns and He pleads and He waits
    to save
  The many — not just the few —
But some day His patience will have
    expired —
  Say, will it hold out for you?

God's mercy and love are wonderful,
  So tender that heart divine.
'Tis not in His plan that a single soul
  In hell should be left to pine.
This human family He yearns to save;
  He's calling, my friend, to you.
But we know that some day He will call
    no more —
  Will His patience hold out for you?

God's Spirit, He says, will not always
    strive
  On earth, in the hearts of men.
How grateful, my friend, you should be
    today
  That you still hear His pleadings then.
Some day, oh how sad, you will know no
    more
  That patience and love so true.
O sinner, today make your peace with
    Him,
  While His patience holds out for you!
                    Edythe Johnson

CHOOSE

Choose you this day whom you will
　serve,
Choose on whose side you will stand;
Will you stand with the throng,
Who uphold the wrong,
Or be led by the nail-pierced hands?

Consider the wages, tally the cost,
If to Satan's dark paths you should stray;

How tragic if all of God's blessings be
　lost,
And eternal damnation your pay!

So hasten to join in the battle for truth,
Take a stand for the Saviour today;
Surrender to Jesus your talents, your
　youth,
Much is lost each hour you delay!

Verna Bishop

Service

KEEP SWEET

There's a little secret
Worth its weight in gold,
Easy to remember —
Easy to be told;
Changing into blessing
Every curse we meet,
Turning hell into heaven;
This is all — *keep sweet.*

Make us kind and gentle,
Harmless as a dove;
Giving good for evil,
Meeting hate with love:
What though trials press us,
What though tempest beat,
Naught can move or harm us,
If we just — *keep sweet.*

Sweet when things are bitter,
Sweet when things are sad,
Giving songs for sighing,
Making others glad:
In the quiet household,
On the bustling street;
Everywhere and always,
Jesus, *keep me sweet.*

PRAY—GIVE—GO

Three things the Master hath to do,
　And we who serve Him here below,
And long to see His kingdom come,
　Must pray, or give, or go.

He needs them all — the open hand,
　The willing feet, the asking heart —
To work together and to weave
　The threefold cord that shall not part.

Nor shall the giver count his gift
　As greater than the worker's deed,
Nor he in turn his service boast
　Above the prayers that voice the need.

Not all can go; not all can give
　To arm the others for the fray;
But young or old, or rich or poor
　Or strong or weak — we all can pray;

Pray that the full hands open wide
　To speed the message on its way;
That those who hear the call may go,
　And — pray that other hearts may
　　pray.

Annie Johnson Flint

123

STIR ME

Stir me, O stir me, Lord, I care not how,
But stir my heart in passion for the
world;
Stir me to give, to go, but most to pray;
Stir till the blood-red banner be un-
furled
O'er lands that still in heathen darkness
lie,
O'er deserts where no cross is lifted high.

Stir me, O stir me, Lord, till all my heart
Is stirred in strong compassion for
these souls,
Till Thy compelling "must" drives me to
prayer;
Till Thy constraining love reach to the
poles,
Far north and south in burning, deep
desire;
Till east and west are caught in love's
strong fire.

Stir me, O Lord, Thy heart has stirred
By love's intensest fire, till Thou didst
give
Thine only Son, Thy best-beloved One,
E'en to the dreadful cross that I might
live;
Stir me to give myself back to Thee
That Thou canst give Thyself again
through me.

Stir me, O stir me, Lord, for I can see
Thy glorious triumph day begin to
break;
The dawn already gilds the eastern sky.
Oh, church of Christ, awake, awake.
Oh, stir us, Lord, as heralds of that day,
The night is past, our King is on His
way.

IF I GO NOT, PRAY NOT, GIVE NOT

If I go not . . . to those who have not
heard;
If I withhold from them God's precious
Word;
If sin-cursed heathen go to Christless
graves
And never, never know that Jesus saves;
If by my negligence some souls are lost
Despite God's mercy and Calvary's un-
told cost;
If I care not for those in distant lands,
Shall not their blood-guilt be upon my
hands?

If I pray not . . . for those who witness
bear;
If I no intercessory burden share;
If God's dear servants ne'er are in my
heart,
And in their labors, I have no part;
If by my prayerlessness there comes an
hour,
When they lack wisdom, or grace, or
strength, or power
And captive souls escape not sin's strong
bands,
Shall not their blood-guilt be upon my
hands?

If I give not . . . and by my selfishness
I cause God's work and workers sore
distress;
If my poor stingy heart will hardened be
To needs of others, their necessity;
If by my failure some shall never hear
The message of salvation, then I fear
Mine is the sin, and justice fair demands
That I accept the guilt of bloody hands!

THE VINEYARD

There are many who go to the Vineyard
  To answer the call of the Lord,
With an eye not alone to the labor
  But looking for great rewards.
They will work with a zest near the
    highway
  Where those passing by can see
But will drop from the ranks in a moment
  If placed in obscurity.

Yet, the vines at the back of the Vineyard
  Were set out with equal care
And the Master has never forgotten
  How many He planted there.
And the Lord who has called us to labor
  Knows best what each man can do
So be quick to go out in the Vineyard
  Though few may notice you.

For the grapes at the back of the Vine-
    yard
  May grow on the precious stalk
That the Lord would not put near the
    roadside
  Where the thieves and the thoughtless
    walk.
And the place where He bids you to labor
  May seem a forsaken plot
But prove out in the plan of the Master
  A specially *cherished spot!*

Then go out to the place He has given
  Nor question His high decree
But be true to your task till the end time
  Though few may know or see
And the grapes on your side of the Vine-
    yard
  May prove to be Eshol's brand
When the labor is done and the workers
  Before Him, shall stand.

MARY AND MARTHA

Mary was busy and hurried,
  Serving the Friend divine,
Cleansing the cups and the platters,
  Bringing the bread and the wine;
But Martha was careful and anxious,
  Fretted in thought and in word,
She had no time to be learning
  While she was serving the Lord,
For Martha was "cumbered" with serving
  Martha was "troubled" with "things"—
Those that would pass with the using—
  She was forgetting her wings.

But Mary was quiet and peaceful,
  Learning to love and to live,
Mary was learning His precepts,
  Mary was letting Him give —
Give of the riches eternal,
  Treasures of mind and of heart;
Learning the mind of the Master,
  Choosing the better part.
Do we ever labor at serving
  Till voices grow fretful and shrill,
Forgetting how to be loving,
  Forgetting how to be still?

Do we strive for "things" in possession,
  And toil for the perishing meat,
Neglecting the one thing needful —
  Sitting at Jesus' feet?
Service is good when He asks it,
  Labor is right in its place,
But there is one thing better —
  Looking up into His face;
There is so much He would tell us,
  Truths that are precious and deep;
This is the place where He wants us,
  These are the things we can keep.

            Annie Johnson Flint

LABOR NOT IN VAIN

My dishes went unwashed today,
　I didn't make the bed,
I took God's hand and followed
　To Sunday school instead.

O yes, we went adventuring,
　My young people and I,
Explaining in the Bible,
　The truths none can deny.

That my house was neglected,
　That I didn't sweep the stair,
In twenty years no one on earth
　Will know, or even care.

But that I've helped a girl or boy,
　In Christian witness grow,
In twenty years, the whole wide world
　May look and see and know.

NOT ONE IS TURNED AWAY FROM GOD

Not one is turned away from God,
　Not one will He deny;
So let us lead the lost to Him,
　That not one soul may die!
Our weapons are the swords of faith
　And love and fervent prayer,
With time and talents, and the means
　To send the Gospel there.

Not one is turned away from God,
　But if they do not hear
How can they turn to Him, from their
　Tormenting sin and fear?
No, not one soul will He deny,
　But if we do not go
How can they hear the Word of God,
　That One who loves them so?

We, by our prayer, and by our means,
　Can spread the gospel seed,
And countless ransomed souls will find
　The answer to their need;
The darkened lands will fill with light
　By God's redeeming grace,
And we, with them one day shall stand
　Before Him, face to face!

Dorothy Conant Stroud

TAKE YOUR PLACE

Somewhere the world has a place for you
　That is all your own;
Somewhere is work that your hand
　can do,
　And yours alone.
Whether afar over land and sea
　Or close at your door may the duty be,
It calls for your service full and free —
　Take your place!

Somewhere the world has bitter tears
　Your smile might dry;
Somewhere burdened with doubts and
　fears,
　The hopeless sigh.
There are steps that falter, weary, weak,
　For strong, brave arm they vainly seek;
Will you pass them by on the journey
　bleak?
　Take your place!

Somewhere the world has a desert spot
　Your toil might till;
Somewhere a life whose loveless lot
　Your love might fill.
If the place that waits be high or low,
　Question not, cry not, onward go!
The world's great battle needs every
　blow —
　Take your place!

FATHER, TEACH ME

"Father, teach me how to pray,
Tell me what I ought to say,
I would pray like Jesus.

"Father, teach me how to live,
I to Thee my best would give,
I would live like Jesus.

"Father, teach me how to serve,
And Thy holy will observe,
I would serve like Jesus."

Walter M. Lee

MISSIONS

There are many desert places,
Far beyond the sea,
Where the unenlightened races
Hunger for the gospel plea.
To those far-off wildernesses,
Long with vices overgrown,
God the Father sends, and blesses
Ministers to save His own.

If we cannot go there, preaching
Jesus who was crucified,
We can send a message, teaching
That for them a Saviour died.
We can help to lift the sorrow
From some brother in despair;
We can help to make the morrow
Of some sister bright and fair.

There are souls in many regions
Round about us, famishing
For the Bread of Life, and legions
Know not Jesus as their King.
If we cannot go and feed them,
We can lend a helping hand,
Send a messenger to lead them,
And fulfill the Lord's command.

Let us give in fullest measure
As the Lord has prospered each;
Let us open heart and treasure
As the Holy Scriptures teach.
Let us send the proclamation
That the Word of Life is free
To the sons of God's creation,
Both at home and o'er the sea.

BE FRIENDLY

You may not stand in the halls of fame
With honor to thy name;
You may not own a lot of wealth,
Nor even have the best of health;
You may not reach some earthly throne,
Nor claim a palace of your own;
You may not master some great art,
Nor rank with those the world calls smart,
But you can be friendly.

You may not be a scholar great,
Nor with the learned highly rate;
You may not wear a pretty face,
Nor fill a great, important place;
You may not write a book or a song,
Nor have the praises of a throng;
You may not ride in pullman cars,
Nor reach through eloquence the stars,
But you can be friendly.

Yes, friendly with the folks at home,
And friendly where you chance to roam;
Quite friendly all along the way
With those you meet from day to day;
For people know it's well worth while
To wear a kind and friendly smile,
And reach to them a friendly hand,
However great or small they stand —
Yes, you can be friendly.

Walter E. Isenhour

127

SOMETHING YOU CAN DO

If you cannot speak like angels,
If you cannot preach like Paul,
You can tell the love of Jesus,
And say He died for all.

If you cannot rouse the wicked
With the judgment dread alarms,
You can lead the little children
To the Saviour's waiting arms.

Let none hear you idly saying,
"There's nothing I can do."
While souls of men are dying,
And the Master calls for you.

Take the task He gives you gladly,
Let His work thy pleasure be,
Answer quickly when he calleth,
"Here am I, send me, send me."

THIS I CAN DO

I cannot speak to crowds;
I can to one,
And tell him what for me
The Lord hath done.

I like to think that He,
Whose love I tell,
Spoke to one needy heart
By Jacob's well.

When Philip's feet were led
To one strange tryst,
He showed one seeking soul
The seeking Christ.

If 'mid the ones and twos
My work shall be,
Gladly will I fulfill
This ministry.

Some many talents have.
I have but one;
Yet I with them may share
The King's "well done!"

H. T. Lefevre

OPERATION — SOULS

Will you lend your eyes to Christ
  To weep for the souls of men
Will you give your heart to earnest
  prayer
  To save a soul from sin?
Will you cause your feet to walk the way
  Some sin-burdened soul hath trod?
Will you thrust forth a hand to guide
  and lead
  That wretched soul to God?

Remember friend, God's Word hath said,
  With fear this work to do,
Lest we should fail this God-given task
  And other things pursue,
With trembling heart but purpose firm
  The Word of God in hand —
This call to you goes forth today
  To rally to the man.

CREDIT

What care I who gets the credit?
  Only let the work be done;
Christ Himself will handle credits
  With the setting of the sun.
Praise or blame, what does it matter?
  Rise above them every day;
Soul, you'll never win the battle
  If you fear what men will say.
While the world is sick and waiting
  For the something I can be,
Help me, Lord, in stress and struggle
  Just to keep my eyes on Thee.

IN HIS SERVICE

For you who are seeking to serve with
  your best
The Saviour who died that the world
  might be blessed.
Your work in His vineyard can bring
  life anew,
For souls are the harvest, but workers are
  few.

Not fretting if life with its years passing
  by
Has cost you all riches, untreasured on
  high,
But earnestly, prayfully, spreading the
  Word,
Travailing lest someone, somewhere,
  hasn't heard.

Surrendered, obedient, seeking His will
With faith that all needs for your life
  He will fill,
For Jesus, our Shepherd, is King of the
  fold;
Content in His love, you will never grow
  old.
                              Clarence E. Clar

CALL TO CONFLICT

Grant, Lord, that through the printed
    page
  Thy Word will yet be spread
To every nation, race, and tribe,
  Which now in sin is dead.
Oh, let not Satan's lies be sown
  Among the literate;
But let Thy Word to them be given
  Who for the Truth await.
Arise, O Lord, and let Thy Church
  Be victor in the field.

Teach every Christian warrior
  His heavenly sword to wield.
Sound forth Thy trumpet loud and clear,
  Thy sleeping church awake;
Teach us to sacrifice our best,
  And every effort make.

YOU WILL FIND A JOY IN SERVICE

When the blessed Saviour calls you
  You must then prepare to go,
Though it be to steaming jungles
  Or the Northland's ice and snow.

He will ask but what is needed,
  For He knows all things to be;
When He speaks, then answer quickly
  His kind, tender "Follow Me."

In His steps is joy forever,
  By His side is peace untold;
Though you walk through troubled waters
  His sure hand will safe-uphold.

Then, forsaking all things gladly,
  That you may His bidding do,
You will find a joy in service
  That will bless the world and you!
                         Dorothy Conant Stroud

MY INFLUENCE

My life shall touch a dozen lives
  Before this day is done,
Leave countless marks of good or ill,
  E'er sets the evening sun.
This, the wish I always wish,
  The prayer I always pray;
Lord, may my life help others lives,
  It touches by the way.

HUMBLE SERVICE

If you can make life brighter
  For just one soul each day;
If you can bring some sunshine
  Into someone's dark way;
If you by word or action
  Can make one life less drear,
Someone will be the better
  Because God placed you here.

If you can speak of Jesus
  To just one erring heart;
If you to someone downcast
  Fresh courage can impart;
If you by word or action
Can lessen someone's pain,
Or bring some soul to Jesus,
  You will not live in vain.
             Lillian G. Heard

DON'T TELL ME

Don't tell me what you will do
  When you have time to spare;
Tell me what you did today
  To ease a load of care.
Don't tell the dreams you have
  Of conquest still afar;
Don't say what you hope to be,
  But tell me what you are.

Smoking — Drinking

A WHISKY SONG

Sing a song of whisky,
  A pocket without pence;
A purse that's always empty.
  A head that has no sense
Four and twenty jail birds
  Under lock and key,
Curse the drink that cost them
  The birthright of the free.
When their cells were opened
  Drinking more and more:
A drunkard's life behind them,
  A drunkard's life before.
The brewer in his counting house
  Is counting out his money;
The barman in his parlor
  Is eating others' honey.
While starving little children,
  And women lean and poor,
In rags and broken hearted,
  Beg from door to door.
Sing a song of whisky,
  Sound it all the time;
The horrid song of whisky —
  Sorrow, sin and crime.

THE BAR

A bar to heaven, a door to hell,
  Whoever named it, named it well.
A bar to manliness and wealth;
  A door to want and broken health.

A bar to honor, pride and fame;
  A door to grief and sin and shame.
A bar to hope, a bar to prayer;
  A door to darkness and despair.

A bar to honored, useful life;
  A door to brawling, senseless strife.
A bar to all that's true and brave;
  A door to every drunkard's grave.

A bar to joys that home imparts;
  A door to tears and aching hearts.
A bar to heaven, a door to hell;
  Whoever named it, named it well.
          Written by a life convict
          in Joliet prison

MAN HAS NO SMOKESTACK

If God ever had intended,
When He first created man,
That he'd have smoked,
He'd have built him on
An entirely different plan,
He'd have furnished him with
A stovepipe, a damper, and a grate,
And He'd have had a smoke consumer
That was strictly up to date.

I have walked in sunny meadows
Where the sunbeams flashed and broke,
But I never saw the sheep, cattle and
    horses smoke.
I have watched the birds with wonder
When the grass with dew was wet,
But I never saw a robin
Puffing a cigarette.

I have fished in many a river
Where the sucker crop was ripe,
But I never saw a catfish
Puffing a briar pipe.
Man is the only living creature
That parades this vale of tears
Like a smoking traction engine
Puffing smoke from nose and ears.

SAID THE WHISKY FLASK

Said the whisky flask to a cigarette,
"I'd like to make a good sized bet
That I can get more scalps than you,
Although your victims aren't so few."
Said the cigarette to the whisky flask,
"Well, that's easy as I could ask,
For I give the kids their downward start,
Then you pitch in and do your part.
They come to you with a burning thirst,
But I'm the fellow that sees them first
So most of the fellows count on me.
I'll take the bet, it's a cinch do-ye see?"
Then the whisky flask has this to say,
"I never looked at the thing that way
But I confess you spoke the truth.
'Tis you who tackles the foolish youth
You fill his system with dopey smoke,
I mold him into a first class soak;
We work together far too well
To quarrel for even a little spell."
So the whisky flask and the cigarette
Shook hands together and offered a bet,
And away they sauntered side by side
Hunting for victims far and wide:
In every corner of the nation,
Partners in crime and ruination.
So here's our warning, on the level,
Shun them as you would shun the devil.

Stewardship

YOUR MONEY AND MINE

Use your money while you're living —
    Do not hoard it to be proud;
You can never take it with you —
    There is no pocket in a shroud.

Gold can help you on no farther
    Than the graveyard where you lie;

'Though you are rich while living,
    You're a pauper when you die.

Use it, then, some lives to brighten,
    As through life they wearily plod;
Place your bank account in heaven,
    And grow rich toward your God.

131

A DOLLAR I GAVE

Three thousand for my brand new car,
  Five thousand for a piece of sod,
Ten thousand I paid to begin a house —
  A dollar I gave to God.

A tidy sum to entertain
  My friends in pointless chatter,
And when the world goes crazy mad
  I ask, "Lord, what's the matter?"

Yet, there is one big question,
  For the answer I still search
"With things so bad in this old world,
  What's holding back my church?"

OUT OF THIS LIFE

Out of this life I shall never take
  Things of silver and gold I make.
All that I cherish and hoard away
  After I leave, on this earth must stay.
Though I have toiled for a painting rare
  To hang on the wall, I must leave it
    there.
Though I call it mine, and boast its worth
  I must give up when I leave this earth.
All that I gather, and all that I keep
  I must leave behind when I fall asleep.
And I often wonder what I shall own
  In that other life, when I pass alone.
What shall they find, and what
  Shall they see, in the soul that
Answers the call for me?
  Shall the great judge learn
When my task is through,
  That my spirit has gained some riches
    too?
Or shall at last, it be mine to find
  That all I'd worked for is left behind?

WE GIVE THEE BUT THINE OWN

We give Thee but Thine own,
  Whate'er the gift may be;
All that we have is Thine alone,
  A trust, O Lord, from Thee.

May we Thy bounties thus
  As stewards true receive,
And gladly, as Thou blessest us,
  To Thee our first fruits give.

William Walsham How

TO PLEDGE OR NOT TO PLEDGE

To pledge or not to pledge —
  That is the question.
Whether 'tis nobler in a man
  To take the Gospel free
  And let another foot the bill,
Or sign a pledge and pay toward
  Church expense!
To give, to pay — aye, there's the rub
  To pay —
When on the free-pew plan a man
  May have
A sitting free and take the Gospel, too
  As though he paid, and none be aught
  The wiser
Save the church committee who —
  Most honorable men — can keep a
    secret !
"To err is human," and human, too, to
    buy
  At cheapest rate. I'll take the Gospel
    so !
For others do the same — a common rule !
I'm wise; I'll wait, not work —
  I'll pray, not pay,
And let the other fellow foot the bills,
And so I'll get the Gospel free,
  You see !

Sunday School

A SUNDAY SCHOOL TEACHER SPEAKS

This child that God has given you
  Is your special pride and joy,
And you would give your very life
  For this precious girl or boy.

You teach him to be truthful —
  To be honest, to be fair.
When his health or life's in danger
  You're the very first to care.

Never would you dream of shirking
  Your responsibility
In schooling or companionship
  Or sports ability.

But what about his precious soul?
  Do you care for it as much?
Do you teach him of the wonder
  Of the Saviour's blessed touch?

Is this duty left to others
  In an hour or two each week,
When it would be better daily
  If his parent learned to speak?

If we all could work together —
  Parents, teachers — with the Lord,
How those little souls would blossom
  With the message of God's Word!

For the Word of God — the Bible —
  Is your child's most precious tool.
Will you help him learn to use it
  In your home and Sunday school?

THE TEACHER SEES A BOY

His trousers are torn, rolled up to the
  knee,
A hole in his shirt which he caught on a
  tree;
But I see a soul for whom Jesus has died
Clothed in His righteousness, pressed to
  His side.

I see not labor and hours of prayer
Spent for that freckle-faced, naughty boy
  there.
But I see a Saviour with arms open wide
Waiting in heaven to take him inside.

I see not freckles, but man fully grown,
A heart filled with God's Word I've fully
  sown
A life speaking forth for the Saviour
  each day —
O Lord, for this boy I most earnestly
  pray.

I see not mischief, but energy bent
Put to the task where the Lord wants
  it spent;
O God, make this lively, mischievous boy
A power for Thee, to Thy heart a joy.

Margaret Morningstar

133

Thanks

ARE WE THANKFUL?

Are we being fair, I wonder,
  With our Saviour and our Lord?
Do we call upon Him often as He
  Bids us in His Word?
Do we ever kneel before Him in
  The stillness of the night,
Giving thanks when through some
  Trial He has guided us aright?

We may pray to Him at dawning
  For a day of love and peace.
Living through the sunny hours
  When our troubles seem to cease.
Do we kneel again at evening when
  The day is spent and done
And recount these hours to Him,
  Giving thanks for everyone?

If we prayed to Him at evening for
  A night of quiet rest,
Did we thank Him in the morning
  When he granted our request?
If we asked of Him some folly in
  A prayer we thought was just
Did we come when He denied it
  And repledge to Him our trust?

Though He knows our every action,
  Thoughtlessness can grieve Him, too,
Let Him share our joys and sorrows
  As a Friend has right to do.
Let us never be so busy nor so
  Weary of the Way
That we cannot pause to thank Him
  For the blessings of today.

MERCIES AND BLESSINGS

"Loaded with benefits daily,"
Sent from the Father above;
Mercies and blessings abounding,
Gifts of His marvelous love.

Daily the Lord is my Keeper,
Daily He's taking my part,
Daily for me interceding,
Bearing my cause on His Heart.

Strength for the day He supplieth,
Daily He meets every need;
Bears every burden arising,
He is my Shepherd indeed!

THANKSGIVING

For morning sun and evening dew,
For every bud that April knew,
For storm and silence, gloom and light,
And for the solemn stars at night;
For fallow field and burdened byre,
For roof-tree and the hearth-side fire;
For everything that shines and sings,
For dear, familiar daily things —
The friendly trees, and in the sky
The white cloud-squadrons sailing by;
For hope that waits, for faith that dares
For patience that still smiles and bears,
For love that fails not, nor withstands;
For healing touch of children's hands,
For happy labor, high intent,
For all life's blessed sacrament,
O Comrade of our nights and days,
Thou givest all things, take our praise!
                              Arthur Ketchum

134

THANKS TO GOD

"In everything give thanks: for this is the will of God in Christ Jesus concerning you" (I Thessalonians 5:18).

Thanks to God for my Redeemer;
Thanks for all Thou dost provide;
Thanks for times now but a mem'ry;
Thanks for Jesus, by my side;
Thanks for pleasant, balmy springtime;
Thanks for dark and dreary fall,
Thanks for tears by now forgotten;
Thanks for peace within my soul.

Thanks for prayers that Thou hast answered,
Thanks for what Thou dost deny!
Thanks for storms that I have weathered,
Thanks for all Thou dost supply!
Thanks for pain, and thanks for pleasure,
Thanks for comfort in despair,
Thanks for grace that none can measure,
Thanks for love beyond compare.

Thanks for roses by the wayside,
Thanks for thorns their stems contain!
Thanks for home and thanks for fireside,
Thanks for hope, that sweet refrain.
Thanks for joy and thanks for sorrow,
Thanks for heavenly peace with Thee,
Thanks for hope in the tomorrow,
Thanks through all eternity.

J. A. Hultman

BE THANKFUL

When you ask God in the morning
For His guidance through the day,
Thank Him for the many blessings
He in love has sent your way.
When you're asking aid from Heaven
Mingle with your morning prayer

A word of praise and gratitude
For all His kindly care.

When you send up your petition
To the Throne of Grace on High,
Thank Him for the many favors
That His mercy does supply,
Be more mindful of the blessings
That His kindness does impart
And the Lord will doubly bless you
For the joy you brought His heart.

Mark Bullock

THANKSGIVING

Once again our glad thanksgivings
Rise before our Father's throne,
As we try to count the blessings
Of the years so swiftly flown;
As we trace the wondrous workings
Of His wisdom, pow'r and love,
And unite our "Holy! Holy!"
With the seraphim above.

As we gather 'round our firesides
On this new Thanksgiving Day
Time would fail to count the blessings
That have followed all the way;
Grace sufficient, help and healing,
Prayer, oft answered at our call,
And the best of all our blessings,
Christ Himself, our All in All!

While we love to count the blessings —
Grateful for the year that's gone,
Faith would sweep a wider vision,
Hope would gaze yet farther on;
For the signals, all around us,
Seem with one accord to say:
Christ is coming soon to bring us
Earth's last, best Thanksgiving Day!

A. B. Simpson

135

THANK THEE, LORD

Lord, we thank Thee for affliction
  How it draws our hearts to Thee!
Though the road be hard and thorny
  Yet Thy face we still can see.

Thank Thee, Lord, for every trial
  Though we do not understand,
Lead us gently step by step
  And hold us by Thy hand.

Alone, we are most needy and
  No worthiness possess;
In Christ we find our All in All,
  Our strength, our righteousness.

We hear Thy kind, constraining voice
  That bids us trust in Thee,
And only in Thy strength we find
  Our all-sufficiency.

Though all of life seems hopeless, still
  God's faithfulness remains;
Thy Holy Word has bathed our hearts —
  Thy precious peace sustains.

Georgia B. Adams

THANKFUL HEART

I lift my heart to Thee, O God,
  In gratitude and praise
For all Thy blessings of the past,
  And those of future days —
For well I know if I shall live,
  Thy blessings still shall flow
Across my soul in greater joy
  Than I could ever know.
I thank Thee for my faithful friends,
  For sunshine and the rain,
And every blessing hid or seen,
  Though some may come through pain.
O God, accept my thanks to Thee
  Each time I come to pray,
And grant each day that I shall live
  Will be Thanksgiving Day.

F. W. Davis

IN EVERY THING GIVE THANKS

'Mid sunshine, cloud or stormy days,
When hope abounds or care dismays,
When trials press and toils increase
Let not thy faith in God decrease —
  "In every thing give thanks."

All things we know shall work for good,
Nor would we change them if we could;
'Tis well if only He commands;
His promises will ever stand —
  "In every thing give thanks."

He satisfies the longing heart,
He thwarts the tempter's cruel dart,
With goodness fills the hungry soul,
And helps us sing when billows roll.
  "In every thing give thanks."

AN EVENING PRAYER

Dear God, another day is done
And I have seen the golden sun
Swing in the arch from east to west
And sink behind the pines to rest.
I thank Thee that Thou gavest me
The power of sight that I may see
The tinted glories of Thy skies,
An earthly glimpse of paradise;
The power to hear the evening breeze
Swelling in organ harmonies;
The power to feel the tender grasp
Of loving hands in friendship's clasp;
I thank Thee for these gifts to me,
But one thing more I ask of Thee;
From out Thy bounteous, gracious hand
Give me the power to understand,
To understand — to sympathize —
To note the pain in other's eyes;
To have the power rightly to read
The kindly motive of each deed.
And this I humbly ask of Thee
Because I know Thou lovest me.

Tongue — Temper

GUARD THY TONGUE

Guard thou thy tongue from ceaseless
    words,
    Whatever else you do;
And ere you speak of anything,
    Be sure you know it's true.
For oftentimes some little word,
    Though said in fun and jest,
Will fill some tender, loving heart
    With dire unhappiness.

Guard thou thy tongue from careless
    words,
    For frequently I've found
An evil word will gather weight
    When lightly passed around;
So let your mind no evil think,
    Your eyes no evil see,
And when you of your neighbor speak,
    Use words of charity.

Alice M. Barr

M-Y T-E-M-P-E-R

Once I lost my temper,
    Threw it quite aside,
Oh, I did not realize,
    Part of me had died.

Oh, I did not realize,
    That swift anger's fire,
Burns the heart that reaches
    Toward the sky — and higher.

Once I kept my temper,
    When things tried my soul;
Kept it sweet and shining,
    Wonderful and whole.

Then — and this is truthful —
    All the way I trod,
Seemed to lead me brightly,
    Toward the throne of God.

Too Busy

STOP A MINUTE!

No time to read, no time to pray,
No time to serve the Lord today,
No time to teach in Sunday school,
No time — for life is very full.

No time to give a gospel tract,
No time to do a kindly act,
No time to seek as Jesus sought,
No time — for life is very short.

No time to call upon a friend,
No time, e'en though he's near the end,
No time to share another's care,
No time — for life is such a tear.

No time? How much is spent on self?
How much on gaining worldly wealth?
How much on seeking place and ease?
Do you have time for only these?

NO ROOM

As Joseph knocked upon his door
  The keeper of the inn came out,
And heedless of the woman's plight,
  His answer left no chance for doubt.

"No room," he said, and closed the door;
  "There is no room for you to stay;
"No room," we answer when Christ
    knocks
Our hearts uncaring, still, today.

No room for him in busy hours,
  No room amid life's throng;
No room for Christ, the light, the hope,
  The giver of life's song!

No room for Him! How can we go
  Unheeding, careless still,
When all of heaven would rejoice
  To do His blessed will?

No room! May our repentant hearts
  Respond this day and hour,
That Christ, the King of glory may
  Come in His mighty power!

"No room," again we shall repeat —
  "No room for aught but Him!"
Then oh, the glory we shall know
  Which cannot wane or dim!
      Dorothy Conant Stroud

CROWDED OUT

My day was filled with many things,
  Some that I cared a lot about,
For I had planned each moment full,
  But my Lord was crowded out.

I really meant to read His Word,
  To pray with heart devout —

But *things* just crowded in until
  My Lord was crowded out.

For things I wanted most to do
  The time I found, without a doubt.
And somehow days were oft the same:
  My Lord was crowded out.

My heart grew sad without His smile;
  The foe was hard to rout;
For He alone who's all in all
  My heart had crowded out.

At last I've learned to plan 'round Him
  Though friends may plead and pout;
And days are doubly full and rich
  Since He's not crowded out.
      Florence White Willett

COULD YOU SPARE SOME TIME FOR JESUS?

Could you spare some time for Jesus
  Who had time to die for you?
You may say, "I am too busy."
  Yes, but Christ was busy too.

Why not make some time for Jesus
  On Wednesday night each week?
For I'm sure that God will bless you
  With the things that you now seek.

If as Jesus' blood-bought children
  We ignore His urgent call,
How can we expect the heathen
  To learn of Adam's fall?

If we would only come to Jesus
  In thanksgiving and in prayer.
What answers we could look for
  If on Wednesday you were there.
      Lester Knickman

NO TIME FOR GOD

No time for God
What fools we are, to clutter up
Our lives with common things
And leave outside heart's gate
The Lord of Life and Life itself.

No time for God
And soon to say no time
To eat and sleep or love or die.
Take time for God!
Or you shall dwarf your soul
And when the angel Death
Comes knocking at your door
A poor misshapen you will be
To step into eternity.

Someday you'll lay aside
This mortal self and make your way
To worlds unknown
And when you meet Him face to face
Will He — should He
Have time for you?

TOO BUSY

Too busy to read a chapter a day,
Too busy, yes, much too busy to pray,
Too busy to think of your wasted past.
In this whirlwind life which we know
    won't last.

Too busy to speak a word of cheer,
To the heart-broken friend, that stands
    so near.
Too busy to help lift his heavy load,
That he's trying to carry on life's rough
    road.

Too busy gathering a dollar and dime,
For the worthwhile things we haven't
    time.

The devil keeps whispering, "Grab your
    share,
Why waste precious hours in prayer?"

Too busy to heed the orphans cry,
And with a glance we hurry by,
Some day we'll lift our voice to the sky,
For not one of us is too busy to die.

Perhaps when we reach that pearly white
    throne,
God will be too busy to call us His own,
So let us calm down to slower pace,
Be ready to meet Jesus face to face.

FORGETTING GOD

I forgot my Lord in the summertime
    When I was needed the most;
I was not away, but each Lord's Day
    I failed to be at my post.

I forgot my church in the summertime,
    As I lazily lay in bed;
While the faithful few had my work to do,
    And I was spiritually dead.

I forgot my pledge in the summertime,
    When He needed it most of all;
While my cash was spent I was pleasure
    bent,
    "Off duty" for God until fall.

If my Lord should come in the summer-
    time,
    When from duty to God I'm free,
Oh, what would I do when my life is
    through
    If perchance my God should forget me?

J. E. Harvey

139

Testimony

IF JESUS CAME TO YOUR HOUSE

If Jesus came to your house to spend a
day or two,
If He came unexpectedly, I wonder what
you'd do.

Oh, I know you'd give your nicest room
to such an honored Guest,
And all the food you'd serve to Him
would be the very best —

And you would keep assuring Him you're
glad to have Him there,
That serving Him in your home is joy
beyond compare!

But when you saw Him coming, would
you meet Him at the door,
With arms outstretched in welcome to
your Heavenly Visitor?

Or would you have to change your clothes
before you let Him in,
Or hide some magazines and put the
Bible where they'd been?

Would you turn off the radio and hope
He hadn't heard —
And wish you hadn't uttered that last,
loud, hasty word?

Would you hide your worldly music and
put some hymn books out?
Could you let Jesus walk right in, or
would you rush about?

And I wonder — if the Saviour spent a
day or two with you —

Would you go right on doing the things
you always do?

Would you keep right on saying the
things you always say?
Would life for you continue as it does
from day to day?

Would your family conversation keep up
its usual pace?
And would you find it hard each meal to
say a table grace?

Would you sing the songs you always sing
and read the books you read,
And let Him know the things on which
your mind and spirit feed?

Would you take Jesus with you everywhere you'd planned to go,
Or would you, maybe, change your plans
for just a day or so?

Would you be glad to have Him meet
your very closest friends,
Or would you hope they'd stay away until
His visit ends?

Would you be glad to have Him stay for-
ever on and on,
Or would you sigh with great relief when
He at last was gone?

It might be interesting to know the things
that you would do
If Jesus came in person to spend some
time with you.

140

HOW DO YOU LIVE?

I'd rather see a sermon than to hear it
  any day.
I'd rather one walk with me than just
  to show the way.
The eye's a better pupil and more willing
  than the ear.
Advice may be misleading, but an example's always clear.
And the very best of preachers are the
  men who live their creeds.
For to see good put into action is what
everybody needs.
I soon can learn to do it, if you'll let me
  see it done.
I can watch your hands in motion, but
  your tongue too fast may run.
And the lectures you deliver may be very
  fine and true,
But I'd rather get my lessons by observ-
  ing what you do.
For I may misunderstand how you act but
  never how you live.

Trust

THE MYSTERIOUS WAY

God moves in a mysterious way
  His wonders to perform;
He plants His footsteps in the sea
  And rides upon the storm.

Deep in unfathomable mines
  Of never-failing skill,
He treasures up His bright designs
  And works His sovereign will.

Ye fearful saints, fresh courage take;
  The clouds ye so much dread
Are big with mercy, and shall break
  In blessings on your head.

Judge not the Lord by feeble sense,
  But trust Him for His grace;
Behind a frowning providence
  He hides a smiling face.

His purposes will ripen fast,
  Unfolding every hour;
The bud may have a bitter taste,
  But sweet will be the flower.

Blind unbelief is sure to err,
  And scan His work in vain;
God is His own interpreter,
  And He will make it plain.

                    William Cowper

PROGRESS

Until I learned to trust,
  I did not learn to pray,
And I did not learn to fully trust
  Till sorrows came my way.
Until I felt my weakness,
  His strength I never knew,
Nor dreamed till I was stricken
  That He would see me through.
Who deepest drinks of sorrow
  Drinks deepest too of grace,
He sends the storm so He Himself
  Can be our hiding place.
His heart that seeks our highest good
  Knows well when things annoy,
We would not long for heaven
  If earth held only joy.

ALL THE WAY MY SAVIOUR LEADS ME

All the way my Saviour leads me;
What have I to ask beside?
Can I doubt His tender mercy,
Who through life has been my Guide?
Heavenly peace, divinest comfort,
Here by faith in Him to dwell!
For I know, whate'er befall me,
Jesus doeth all things well.

All the way my Saviour leads me,
Cheers each winding path I tread,
Gives me grace for every trial,
Feeds me with the living bread.

Though my weary steps may falter,
And my soul athirst may be,
Gushing from the Rock before me,
Lo! a spring of joy I see.

All the way my Saviour leads me;
Oh, the fullness of His love!
Perfect rest to me is promised
In my Father's house above.
When my spirit, clothed immortal,
Wings its flight to realms of day;
This my song thro' endless ages:
Jesus led me all the way.

Fanny J. Crosby

Victory

VICTORY

Long long ago on Calvary,
  There hung upon a cross
A lifeless figure given in love
  To whom was written "loss."

A Roman soldier tough and hard
  Fought back a silent tear,
And women stood and wept aloud
  'Twas more than they could bear.

His words and works were full of love,
  His life a sacrifice,
The mob was as pitiless — the priests
  Triumphant with the price.

But God is love, and righteousness
  Won over worldly strife,
For Jesus Christ arose again
  To everlasting life.

KEEPING VICTORY

Meet your Saviour in the morning
  In the secret place of prayer,
And obtain the strength and courage
  You shall need for ev'ry care.
Meet your loved ones and your neighbors,
  Meet your friends and meet your foes;
Meet the sinners and the Christians
  With sweet peace that overflows.

Meet your trials and your problems,
  Meet your heartaches and your sighs;
Meet your many disappointments,
  And whatever sorely tries,
With a heart of love and kindness
  And with faith that reaches God,
Knowing that His hand will lead you
  Up the way that saints have trod.

Walter E. Isenhour

142

Warning

BUILDING THE BRIDGE FOR HIM

An old man, traveling a lone highway,
Came at the evening cold and gray,
To a chasm deep and wide.

The old man crossed in the twilight dim,
For the sullen stream held no fears for
    him,
But he turned when he reached the other
    side,
And builded a bridge to span the tide.

"Old man," cried a fellow pilgrim near,
"You are wasting your strength with
    building here;
Your journey will end with the ending
    day,
And you never again will pass this way.

"You have crossed the chasm deep and
    wide.
Why build you a bridge at eventide?"
And the builder raised his old gray head:
"Good friend, on the path I have come,"
    he said,
"There followeth after me today
A youth whose feet will pass this way.

"This stream, which has been as naught
    to me,
To that fair-haired boy may a pitfall be;
He, too, must cross in the twilight dim —
Good friend, I am building this bridge
    for him."

W. A. Dromgoole

With Christ

CHRIST ALONE

Oh, the bitter shame and sorrow,
    That a time could ever be
When I let the Saviour's pity
    Plead in vain; and proudly answered,
"All of self, and none of Thee!"

Yet He found me; I beheld Him
Bleeding on the accursed tree;
    Heard Him pray "Forgive them,
        Father!"

And my wistful heart said faintly,
    "Some of self, and some of Thee."

Day by day His tender mercy,
    Healing, helping, full and free;
Sweet and strong, and, ah! so patient,
    Brought me lower, while I whispered,
"None of self, and all of Thee!"

Theodore Monod

CHRIST ALONE

Strange, fantastic claims abound;
　You may hear them all around,
Some have visions, trances, dreams,
　Others — cunning, subtle schemes;
Golden plates or "Bluish flame,"
　"Cosmic rays" — they're all the same;
One thing common do they share:
　(You can tell them anywhere);
Works or money you must pay
　Else "no help for you" they say.

But when from these frauds we turn,
　When for truth and right we yearn;
God will tell you in His Word
　That your faintest prayer is heard;
And you'll know there's only one
　Who can save "beneath the sun."
All the rest impostors be —
　Christ alone can set you free.
He made claims as well. We're sure
　His credentials still endure.

No impostor raised the dead,
　Made the crippled strong instead,
Stilled a storm and calmed a sea,
　Set a demon captive free,
Cleansed the leper from his stain ,
　Gave His life and rose again.
Only one will qualify
　To redeem and justify.

Christ alone can save from sin,
　Trust Him now and enter in.
Shel Helsley

WITH HIM

In the dawn of breaking day,
　When its first faint rays I see,
I can hear my Saviour say,
　"Walk this day with Me."

When I feel the noon day's heat,
　I press closer to His side,
There indeed is a retreat,
　There in Him, I can abide.

When the sunset tints the West,
　And the day is done,
He giveth His beloved rest,
　To the weary one.
Julia E. Martin

CHRIST FOR EVERYTHING

Christ for life, and Christ for living,
　Christ for health, and Christ for
　　healing,
Christ for night and Christ for day,
　Christ for all along the way;
Christ the all-sufficient Friend;
　Christ abiding to the end.
R. A. Belsham

Witnessing — Evangelism

NOTHING BETTER

Is there anything else that is better worth,
　As along life's way we plod,
Than to find some wand'ring soul of
　　earth
　And bring him home to God?
I would rather find a soul that is lost,

And bring it home again,
Than to own what all earth's acres cost,
　Or all the wealth of men.
Wouldn't I be glad when the day is done
　In breathing my last breath,
To know some word of mine had won
　And saved a soul from death?

SHINE JUST WHERE YOU ARE

Don't waste your time in longing
  For bright, impossible things;
Don't sit supinely yearning
  For the swiftness of eagles' wings;

Don't spurn to be a rushlight
  Because you are not a star,
But brighten some bit of darkness
  By shining just where you are.

There is need of the tiniest candle
  As well as the garnish sun;
The humblest deed is ennobled
  When it is worthily done;

You may never be called to brighten
  The darkened regions afar;
So fill, for the day, your mission
  By shining just where you are.

WHILE THE DAYS ARE GOING BY

There are lonely hearts to cherish
  While the days are going by;
There are weary souls who perish,
  While the days are going by,
If a smile we can renew,
  As our journey we pursue,
Oh, the good that we may do,
  While the days are going by.

There's no time for idle scorning,
  While the days are going by;
Let your face be like the morning,
  While the days are going by,
Oh, the world is full of sighs,
  Full of sad and weeping eyes;
Help your fallen brothers rise,
  While the days are going by.

All the loving links that bind us
  While the days are going by;
One by one we leave behind us,
  While the days are going by;
But the seeds of good we sow,
  Both in shade and shine will grow,
And will keep our hearts aglow,
  While the days are going by.

SPEAK OUT FOR JESUS

You talk about your business
  Your bonds and stocks of gold;
And in all your worldly matters
  You are so brave and bold.

But why are you so silent
  About salvation's plan?
Why don't you speak for Jesus
  And speak out like a man?

You talk about the weather
  And the crops of corn and wheat.
You speak of friends and neighbors
  That pass along the street.

You call yourself a Christian
  And you like the Gospel plan,
Then why not speak for Jesus
  And speak out like a man?

Are you ashamed of Jesus
  And the story of the cross,
That you lower His pure banner
  And let it suffer loss?

Have you forgot His sufferings?
  Did He die for you in vain?
If not, then live and speak for Jesus
  And speak out like a man.

LIFE'S LITTLE THINGS

'Twas only a cheerful, radiant smile
  He flashed as he hurried along;
But his work less arduous seemed that
    day
  For a heart had been filled with song.

'Twas only a helpful, kindly word
  He paused to speak to the sad;
Yet his steps were light, his hopes were
    high,
  For a life had been helped — made
    glad.

'Twas only a song he whistled or sang
  As he toiled at his morning's task;
To the stranger it gave new courage and
    hope,
  Had he known — what more could he
    ask?

'Twas only a silent, earnest prayer
  That he breathed to his Lord that hour;
Yet the fainting worker, tired and worn,
  Had received new strength and power.

'Twas only a friendly thought of one
  Revealed by a word or prayer;
Yet a heart was made more strong and
    true,
  Does it pay, do you think, just to care?

THE SOUL WINNER'S PRAYER

Oh, give me, Lord, Thy love for souls,
  For lost and wand'ring sheep,
That I may see the multitudes
  And weep as Thou dost weep.
Help me to see the tragic plight
  Of souls far off in sin;
Help me to love, to pray, and go
  To bring the wand'ring in.

146

Take Thou some flaming coals,
  From off the altar of thy heart
To touch my life and give me, Lord,
  A heart that's hot for souls.
O Fire of Love, O Flame Divine,
  Make Thy abode in me;
Burn in my heart, burn evermore,
  Till I burn out for Thee.

Eugene M. Harrison

NOT ON SUNDAY NIGHT

I love the church that Jesus bought,
And know that it is right;
I go there on Sunday morning,
But not on Sunday night.

I love to sing the songs of God,
Such worship must be right,
This I do on Sunday morn,
But not on Sunday night.

God bless the preacher too,
And give him power and might,
But put the sinner in his place,
I won't be there Sunday night.

I love to hear the Gospel too,
It gives me pure delight;
I hear it on Sunday morning,
But not on Sunday night.

I know I need more strength
To keep me in the fight;
For help I come on Sunday morn,
But not on Sunday night.

Yes, we all must die,
I hope I will be right,
So may I die on Sunday morn,
But not on Sunday night.

PRAYER FOR NEIGHBORHOOD EVANGELISM

O Lord, it is not hard to love
The heathen far away,
Who've never heard the blessed Word
The Life, The Truth, the Way;
Whose home is ghastly pagan
With idol worship, Such —
O Lord, our hearts go out to them,
We love them very much.

But 'tis another matter,
The man across the street
Who uses vile language,
And scoffs whene'er we meet,
He dececrates the Lord's Day
And doesn't seem to care.
O Lord, it is for these today
We lift our hearts in prayer.

'Tis true, perhaps they know the Way,
Yet walk in paths of sin,
May we not point the finger
But seek to bring them in.
We need not to show what we have done,
For we have naught to show.
'Tis only Thy great love alone
That these poor souls must know.

O Lord, in this our mission
We fail so miserably;
Forgetting we would be as they
Had it not been for Thee.
O give us greater vision, Lord,
And stir our hearts today
That these be brought into the fold
In Jesus' Name we pray.

Annetta Jansen

Worry

PEACE

O for a heart of calm repose
  Amid the world's loud roar,
A life that like a river flows
  Along a peaceful shore!

Come, Holy Spirit, still my heart
  With gentleness divine;
Indwelling peace thou canst impart:
  O make that blessing mine!

Come, Holy Spirit, breathe that peace,
  That victory make me win;
Then shall my soul her conflict cease,
  And find a heaven within.

FEAR NOT

Sow ye by all waters
  Where the dew of heaven may fall,
Ye shall reap if ye be not weary,
  For the Spirit breathes o'er all.

Fear not, for some will flourish —
  And though the tares abound;
Like the willows by the waters,
  Will the scattered grain be found.

Work while the daylight lasteth,
  Ere the shades of night come on;
Ere the Lord of the vineyard cometh,
  And the laborer's work is done.

J. Bullock

WORRY

A little hope, a lot of faith,
  Are what we need today,
We learn from past experience
  That worry does not pay.

We wring our hands and rack our brain
  In moments of despair.
But all that worry does for us
  Is bring us more gray hair.

For when the things we worry o'er
  Are finally understood,
We do not find them half so bad
  As first we thought we would.

So should our reason deem it wise,
  Our worries we discard,
Then substitute a little hope
  And lots of faith in God.

George W. Swarberg

Worship

WAITING FOR THE MORNING

There is no roof in all the world,
Of palace or of cot.
That hideth not some burdened heart
Nigh breaking for its lot!
The earth is filled with pain and tears,
And closer draws the gloom;
And light or balm there can be none
Till Christ the Lord shall come.

My Saviour, who doth know the thirst
The longing spirit feels —
O Bridegroom, now so long afar,
Why stay thy chariot wheels?
Were ever eyes so dim with tears,
Breasts so oppressed with care?
Did ever hearts so yearn to catch
Thy whisper from the air?

Thou lonely one, lift up thy head;
Array thee for the feast;
He that hath tarried long is near;
The glow is in the east!
O Morning Star, so soon to lead
Thy chosen ones away —
O Sun of Righteousness, bring in
The everlasting day.

GOD'S PRESENCE MAKES MY HEAVEN

God's presence makes my heaven;
Earth's treasures fade and flee;
I'm satisfied with Jesus,
He's ev'rything to me.

I know He will not leave me,
Nor yet forsake me here;
I rest upon His promise
And banish ev'ry fear.

God's presence makes my heaven,
My paradise below,
For He Himself is with me
No matter where I go.

I walk and talk with Jesus
Along life's busy way,
For He is ever near me,
My comfort and my stay.

How could I live without Him,
My Saviour, Friend, and Guide!
His presence makes my heaven
And I am satisfied.

Oswald J. Smith.

148

NO GREATER LOVE

I walked one day on a lonely road,
My soul in deep despair.
I sought in vain to loose the load,
That sin, my sin, had planted there.

When in the distance I perceived,
A man bent low with care.
He bore in agony a cross,
That sin, my sin, had planted there.

I cried aloud as He drew near,
His hands were pierced and torn.
His grief so far outweighed my own,
And I had dared to mourn.

His eyes of love were turned on me,
His voice was soft and free.
"Why bear you still the load I took,
Through death on Calvary?"

"Why, Lord," in awe and shame I cried,
"Didst Thou all this for me?"
His answer I shall ne'er forget,
"Because of love for thee."

Now as the road of time I tread,
My Saviour walks with me.
He bears the load, He paid the price,
That bought me liberty.

O HOW I LOVE THY LAW

O how I love Thy holy law!
   'Tis daily my delight;
And thence my meditations draw
   Divine advice by night.

How doth Thy Word my heart engage!
   How well employ my tongue,
And in my tiresome pilgrimage
   Yields me a heavenly song.

When nature sinks, and spirits droop,
   Thy promises of grace
Are pillars to support my hope,
   And there I write Thy praise.

Isaac Watts

GOD IS WITH ME

On the sea or in the air
God is with me ev'rywhere,
He will never let me go
For I know He loves me so;
Ev'ry day and ev'ry hour
He will keep me by His pow'r.

Oswald J. Smith

BLESSED NEARNESS

The calm of heaven rests upon my heart
When I behold the scenes of nature's art.
There is an unseen presence that
   pervades
The splendor of the mountains, fields,
   and glades.

It is a thing sublime to know God lives
So close to His creation that He gives
The feeling that you're walking hand
   in hand
With Him who made things beautiful and
   grand.

I walk with reverent step these quiet ways
Where every thought is lifted up in
   praise.
His blessed nearness makes my spirit
   whole
And lingers like sweet fragrance in my
   soul.

Mary Bullock

149

Youth

THE FOUR CALLS

The Spirit came in *Childhood*
And pleaded, "Let Me in";
But O the door was bolted
And barred by childish sin.
This child said, "I'm too little;
There's time enough for me;
Today, I cannot open."
The Spirit went away.

Again, He came and pleaded,
In *Youth's* bright, happy hour;
He called, but heard no answer;
For, fettered in sin's power
The youth lay, idly dreaming,
And crying, "Not today;
For I must have some pleasure!"
Again, He turned away.

He came again, in mercy,
In *manhood's* vigorous prime;
But still could find no welcome;
The merchant had no time
To spare for true repentance,
No time to praise and pray;
And thus repulsed and saddened,
The Spirit turned away.

Once more, He called — and waited;
The man was *old* and sad;
He scarcely heard the whisper —
His heart was scarred and bad.
"Go! leave, until I need Thee;

I'll send for Thee," he cried —
Then, sinking on his pillow,
Without a hope, he died.

Lydia Hadley

HAVE COURAGE, MY BOY, TO SAY, NO

You're starting, my boy, on life's journey,
    Along the grand highway of life,
You'll meet with a thousand temptations,
    Each city with evil is rife.
This world is a stage of excitement —
    There's danger wherever you go;
But if you are tempted in weakness,
    Have courage, my boy, to say, No!

The bright, ruby wine may be offered —
    No matter how tempting it be,
From poison it stings like an adder,
    My boy, have courage to flee.
The billiard saloons are inviting,
    Decked out in their tinsel and show,
But if you are tempted to enter —
    Have courage, my boy, to say, No.

In courage alone lies your safety,
    When you the long journey begin;
Your trust in the Heavenly Father
    Will keep you unspotted from sin.
Temptation will keep on increasing
    As streams from a rivulet flow;
But if you'd be true to your manhood,
    Have courage, my boy, to say, No!

GOD'S CALL

Shall I spend the days of my youth in
  pride,
And leave no longing of life denied;
Shall I heap to myself an earthly
  treasure,
And worship before the throne of
  pleasure,
Ambition, and hope, and life are mine,
And dreams as bright as the stars that
  shine.
With empty glamor the world allures,
The devil beckons, the flesh conjures.
Shall I close my heart to the God of
  Truth,
And leave Him out of my years of youth,
Then when I have wasted away the best,
Return to the Father and offer the rest;
A shattered vessel, a few short years,
A life made bitter by selfish fears?

Since God so loved that He gave His all,
Shall I give less when I hear His call?

Oh, no, Lord Jesus, while I am young
To teach Thy Word will I give my
  tongue;
My feet to follow where Thou shalt lead,
My hands to labor for Thee indeed;
And all ambition my heart has known;
I yield to Thee, to be Thine alone.
The plans that selfishly I have made,
With hopes and dreams are before Thee
  laid.
A faithful steward I long to be
Over any talent entrusted me,
That when I face the eternal Son
And He sees His fruit, He may say,
  "Well done."
Oh, take my heart, my life, my all —
I have heard Thy voice, I have met Thy
  call.